Life Hack 101: The Ultimate Guide to College Success!

_By_

Jordan T. Ball

Life hack 101: The Ultimate Guide to College Success

Life Hack 101: The Ultimate Guide to College Success

© 2017 by Jordan T. Ball

Published by Jordan T. Ball

Cover designed at www.canva.com edited by Josh V. Joseph

Any questions ,suggestions or success stories please send to LifeRehab101@gmail.com

LifeRehab101.com

Jordan Ball, P.O. Box 473, Fresno TX, 77545

To the millions of readers of Life Hack 101: The Ultimate Guide to College Success and the thousands that have written me.

Thank you for your feedback, encouraging letters/e-mails, and success stories.

You inspire me to do what I do.

This book is designed and intended to be used by following directly, providing accurate and authoritative information on the subject of college readiness and scholastic success. It is sold with the understanding that neither the Author nor the Publisher is engaged in rendering legal or other professional services by publishing this book. The Author and Publisher specifically disclaim any liability, loss, risk, or failure that is incurred consequently, directly or indirectly, of the use and application of any of the contents of this work.

Life Hack 101: The Ultimate Guide to College Success

1st Edition January 2017

Printed in the United States of America

ISBN: 978-0-692-83462-6 (pbk)

Life Hack 101 is spaced to encourage you to write inside. Use the spaces or blanks to jot down any spur of the moment ideas or thoughts before they are gone. It is my belief that some of the greatest ideas known to man never came to be because someone forgot to write it down. Don't let it happen to you!

Contents

● ● ● ● ● ● ● ● ● ● ●

Contents

•••••••••

"The future is not some place we are going, but one we create. The paths are not found, but made, and the activity of making them changes both the maker and the destination."

-John Schaar-

<u>Dedication</u>

I dedicate this book to every obstacle I have faced and

every NO I ever heard. Thank you for helping to make

me who I am today.

To my mom and dad thank you for having my back,

loving me, and supporting me.

To my sisters thank you for driving me.

To my grandmother thank you for watching over me

from heavens porch.

To Mrs. Thomas thank you for awakening me.

PREFACE:

"We are made wise not by the recollection of our past, but by the responsibility for our future."

-George Bernard Shaw-

My purpose for doing this is because for most, college can seem to be an insurmountable obstacle. My experience was that and more. I have taken many wrong turns and faced challenges no one should have to.

Though the road is rugged, there are some timely small victories. The information you gain while running what may seem to be a marathon is indispensable. This is the playbook I needed and did not have at the time. I learned by experience so that you, the reader, may utilize this blueprint during your journey to success through those troublesome college years. This book is filled with little seeds when fostered can change your life. *Take them. Plant them. Water them. Enjoy the fruit*

What Can College Preparedness Do For You

Imagine how YOU would feel if YOU knew that the moment YOU stepped on your college campus YOU had a pocket full of money, a few friends, and everything else YOU could ever need to be successful in YOUR pursuit of a degree.

For some people this is exactly how the story begins. They have practically no worries when it comes to college, and in four to five years, they graduate and become successful pillars in their respective communities. Most times, with this success, people are magnetically drawn to the people they view as always ready, and feel urged to continuously help these prepared people any way they can.

These prepared people lead lives that are more exciting, work better jobs, gain more opportunities, and in turn make more money. YOUR level of preparedness WILL determine whether YOU are a follower or a leader, whether YOUR ideas are adopted, and ultimately how effectively YOU navigate along YOUR path to success. Being prepped makes people believe in YOU, trust YOUR plans and vision, and want to be led by YOU.

Will Smith an honorary PhD student in the field of performing arts made this comment early on in his career and the rest is history, "So if you stay ready, you ain't gotta get ready, and that's the way I run my life." Being ready as Mr. Smith so eloquently put it is critical in every aspect of your life, especially for college! If you are a leader, desire to be a leader, or want to achieve success in every endeavor, preparation matters!

It's Not Rocket Science

Beyond popular belief those people who excel over others were not innately successful from birth. If this were the case people like Bill Gates, J.K Rowling, Oprah Winfrey, or Colonel Sanders (KFC) would not exist.

Luckily for YOU, this mystery on being prepared has been turned into an applicable knowledge. What this book does is translate the science of college readiness into practical, easy to read, funny, inspirational, and immediately applicable tools with measurable results. You will enjoy the process of learning how to get ready for and stay ready in college in a methodically systematic way.

With the use of inspirational quotation, stories, and practical exercises immediately useful in the real world it won't even feel like YOU are learning and growing. Moreover, unlike those of us who became versed by trial and error, YOU will not have to waste any time figuring out what works and does not work. YOU can go directly to the tried and true tools that really do make YOU into a highly effective student.

The Author's Story

My arduous journey began the summer going into my senior year of high school. I was in summer school to get ahead and graduate a year early. I thought I was something. I was on top of the world. A man, even though I was only sixteen at the time. You couldn't tell me nothing! At least I thought. Until one day, my dad called me into the living room for a conversation that looking back on kind of changed my life. The irony is, my dad has no recollection that this conversation even happened.

Nevertheless, my father proceeds to tell me "Son, you're growing up, and I'm proud of the young man you are becoming. You are going into senior year and should be looking at college stuff soon. When you are looking through these options make sure you pick a major where you can get a real job. I don't want to hear anything about this Theatre stuff, especially if your mom and I are going to be paying for it." Everything that came out of his mouth after that was muffled by the thoughts taking over my mind now. Thoughts like *"But that's what I love! Should I follow my heart or obey my father? What if I don't like what I choose, and the rest of my life is miserable? What do I choose? I don't really know how this college thing works! I never get to make any decisions for my own life. IT'S MY LIFE!"* However, I smiled on the outside and said thank you when really my whole world had been turned upside down on the inside. I understand now that what my dad was doing was only trying to make sure I had a full proof plan in place to where somewhere down the road I could take care of myself.

Following that conversation, I didn't take high school as seriously as I should have. Mainly because I was extremely smart. I was the person who could study one time or the night before the test and make a 100. So, I didn't do homework most times because I knew I would ace the test. That's a big no no; six zeros outweigh a 100 any day. Even though I enjoyed learning and the social environment of high school, like most students I was uninterested. I felt as if schooling was important so I'm not a bum, but at the same time a waste of time. I often asked myself "Why do I need to spend 8 hours a day here when I can cram the night before and make good grades?"

Also moving from different schools or to new cities every few years always having to start over and make new friends didn't help either. Overall, knowing what I know now I should have been way more committed and disciplined myself better in that short time I was in high school.

The time had come for class rankings and GPA's to be given to us. I will never forget I was in fourth period sports marketing, Mr. Barret. They told us not to let anyone see our rankings or GPA's, but as all teenagers would do we immediately started asking around. By the end of that class I realized I was the highest ranked in our class period. I felt accomplished. Still not understanding this concept fully I got to physics where I sat by one of my friends. As our lecture went on, I decided to ask him what his ranking was. I knew I made higher grades than he did and he cheated off me on almost all of the class assignments. I admit I was being petty at the time, but I soon came to find that his class ranking was higher than mine was. How in heaven's gate could this be? I needed answers, but didn't know where to go. This was a new school for me, and a new situation. I talked to my parents who then immediately went to my counselor.

It was at that time we found out indeed that my class ranking was calculated incorrectly. The school had used my unweighted GPA, which did not take into consideration the advanced placement courses I had taken years before at my previous schools. I thought that was the end of it. We are good, I got that taken care of, and life is good now. Nevertheless, it wasn't. I realized I needed my final GPA and class ranking for the college application process. To my surprise, the problem had not been corrected from the original mix up. I was infuriated and devastated all at the same time. I petitioned for a change, but with graduation right around the corner all I got is "There is nothing we can do now. The situation is out of our control since final GPA's and class rankings had already been posted."

This changed everything. I was once a potential full ride college student at any school in the state of Texas and most other schools outside of the state to now barely able to get scholarships for tuition let alone room and board. I came to the realization after much deliberation with my parents that I was most likely going to have to work and go to school. I've always had to be the type of person that adapts to the things that happen in my life so I did just that.

When I got to college, I had a chip on my shoulder based off what happened in high school. I felt like they owed me when in reality NO ONE owes YOU anything. I let that chip rule me instead of fuel me to prove them wrong. This attitude created an avalanche that almost buried me in stress, depression, anxiety, a yearning to feel validated, and just the overall feeling of being lost and out of place.

Throughout my life I always stood out no matter how hard I tried to fly under the radar I just never really fit in. So eventually, I began to act out and seek that validation. My mom in those troublesome years said one thing that really stuck with me. She called me a *"chameleon"*, and that she didn't know who I was at times. It hurt her when she said it, but it hurt me even more. I never wanted to burden my mother. No matter how I tried to dismiss this statement, she was right. With my friends and acquaintances, I was a class clown, a comedian, the life of the party. On the other hand, with my parents, church, and family I was a saint who could do no wrong, very respectful, and sometimes an introvert. Throughout my life, I continued to be a chameleon. Then I grew up, put away those childish things and became a good chameleon that had integrity, goals, never met a stranger, and knew who he was so he never was caught up being something he wasn't.

When I got to college, I did not exactly know what my future had in store for me, and had no earthly idea of how to get to that future. This unsureness coupled with those bad habits I had cultivated in high school almost caused me to become a career college student.

With that being said, don't become a career college student. Finish what you started in a timely matter. At the same time, feel free to stay there as long as YOU NEED to. Just have a plan, and tune out all the naysayers. ***There will always be naysayers no matter how good or bad you do!*** Never forget no matter all the wonderful places will go, everything happens for a reason. Rather it is good, bad, or indifferent. So don't worry if your story is not ideal or like everyone else's. This is the beauty of life that makes all of us unique. The world needs YOUR story. No one else can write it but YOU. I need

YOU and all that YOU have to offer. There **IS** and will only ever be one of YOU **EVER!** So make sure YOU leave a legacy, make YOUR mark, and give us the best version of YOU possible!

Lastly, I went through hell and high water so that hopefully you will not have to. I took the hard road and picked up most everything laid out for you in this book along the way. Some of those things I can account to having great mentors in my life like my parents, other family members, my pastor, and a few outside mentors who already embodied where I thought I wanted to go. Taking into consideration everything that I have learned one of the most important lessons I can sum up in one line,

It is not only YOUR privilege, but also YOUR duty to help others.

"Human behavior flows from three main sources: Desire, Emotion, and Knowledge."
—Plato-

WHAT'S

Your

TC?

Before you start this journey, take this quick True color or TC test. It's used to find out your most dominate personality type, and some characteristics that you may have. On a following page, you will take a True Color test that is going to change your view on life from this day forward. Use this test to help understand and govern how you interact with people. After taking the test and finding out your TC, pair yourself with a person who does not have the same True Color as you in which you think their personality type will benefit you most. This person will act as your accountability partner as well as a differing outlook on life, goals, and YOUR pursuit of success.

Directions: *Reading across in* **ROWS***, in the box rank the* **GROUP** *of words by how they describe you on a scale of 1-4. There* **MUST** *be a 1,2,3, and 4 in each row. #'s should not repeat per row. 1=least likely to describe you and 4=most likely to describe you. When all* **ROWS** *are complete, add up the number in each* **COLUMN** *to get your score for each color!*

Example:

Row

Affectionate	Joyful	Egotistical
_3_	_1_	_2_
Lazy	Organized	Indifferent
_1_	_2_	_3_
Picky	Nonchalant	Overbearing
_3_	_2_	_1_
Total	Total	Total
7	5	6

Column

Orange		Gold		Blue		Green	
Active Opportunistic Spontaneous		Parental Traditional Responsible		Authentic Harmonious Compassion		Versatile Inventive Competent	
Competitive Impetuous Impactful		Practical Sensible Dependable		Unique Empathetic Communicate		Curious Conceptual Knowledge	
Realistic Open-minded Adventurous		Loyal Conservative Organized		Devoted Warm Poetic		Theoretical Seeking Ingenious	
Daring Impulsive Fun		Concerned Procedural Cooperative		Tender Inspirational Dramatic		Determined Complex Composed	
Exciting Courageous Skillful		Orderly Conventional Caring		Vivacious Affectionate Sympathetic		Philosophical Principled Rational	
Total		Total		Total		Total	

BLUE

emotionally driven
seeks harmony in groups
enthusiastic
creative
sympathetic

GOLD

loyalty driven
respects rules and authority
responsible
organized
appreciative

ORANGE

short-term driven
welcomes change and variety
adventerous
competetive
impulsive

GREEN

logically driven
independent thinker
focused
efficient
analytical

*"Personality has power to uplift, **power to depress,** power to curse, and **power to bless."**___ —Paul Harris-*

Gold:

I am conventional. I am the pillar of strength and have high respect for authority. I like to establish and maintain policies, procedures, and schedules. I have a strong sense of right and wrong. I am naturally parental and dutiful. I do things that require organization, dependability, management, and detail. I need to be useful and belong. I am the sensible, stable backbone of any group. I believe that work comes before play. I value home, family, status, security, and tradition. I seek relationships that help me ensure a predictable life. I am caring, concerned, and loyal. I show concern through the practical things I do.

Orange:

I am courageous. I act on a moment's notice. I see life as a roll of the dice, a game of chance. I need stimulation, freedom, and excitement. I am a natural leader, troubleshooter, and performer. I like to do things that require variety, results, and participation. I often enjoy using tools. I am competitive and bounce back quickly from defeat. I value action, resourcefulness, and courage. I am generous, charming, and impulsive. I show affection through physical contact.

Blue:

I am compassionate. I am always encouraging, and supporting. I am a peacemaker, sensitive to the needs of others. I am a natural romantic. I like to do things that require caring, counseling, nurturing, and harmonizing. I have a strong desire to contribute and to help others lead more significant lives. I am poetic and often enjoy the arts. I value integrity and unity in relationships. I am enthusiastic, idealistic, Communicative, and sympathetic. I express my feelings easily.

Green:

I am conceptual. I have an investigative mind, intrigued by questions like, "Which came first, the chicken or the egg?" I am an independent thinker, a natural nonconformist, and live life by my own standards. I like to do things that require vision, problem solving, strategy, ingenuity, design, and change. Once I have perfected an idea, I prefer to move on to a new challenge. I value knowledge, intelligence, insight, and justice. I enjoy relationships with shared interest. I prefer to let my head rule my heart. I am cool, calm, and collected. I do not express my emotions easily.

Other Helpful Test:

Myers Briggs Personality Test

Career Finder Test

Talent & Skills Assessment

True Color Hall of Fame:

Blue:
Ghandi
Oprah
Mozart
Martin Luther King Jr.
Abraham Lincoln
Julius Caesar
Mohammad Ali
President Clinton
Sigmund Freud
Cinderella
Dorothy (Wizard of Oz)

Orange:
Amelia Earhart
JFK
Garfield
Charlie Brown
Teddy Roosevelt
Lucille Ball
Ernest Hemmingway
Winston Churchill

Green:
Carl Jung
Moses
Socrates
Quincy Jones
Thomas Edison
Benjamin Franklin
Sherlock Holmes
Eleanor Roosevelt
Katherine Hepburn

Gold:
Henry Ford
Santa Claus
George Washington
Queen Victoria
Nancy Reagan
The Lone Ranger
Joan Rivers
Florence Nightingale

Interesting stuff right? Just knowing that YOU have so much in common with a few of the world's most influential people should get YOUR creative juices flowing. Use this as a starting point and the lives of the individuals listed to make the necessary adjustments that empower you to be YOUR best! All of the people on this list were not always the brightest or the best, but they were determined to make history, and not just stand around while history is being made. Because rather YOU are involved or not history WILL be made. Take a step off that cliff of life and JUMP to YOUR destiny.

"A journey of a thousand miles begins with one step"

-Lao Tzu-

Part 1:

The

Pre-Game

Warmup

"Success depends upon previous preparation, and without such preparation there is sure to be failure"

-Confucius-

Here is where your life changes for the better. All of

the habits and knowledge that you learn from this point

forward are going to carry you and even keep you afloat

during college. Or maybe even when life is coming at you in a

wave and you just need a buoy. Don't think just because this

stage in your life has passed, or is coming to an end that

you've grasped everything that could have been grasped or in some cases needed. Be the individual who skips through life aware of all the possible beauties that could be right in front of them. Turn over every stone. Take in everything you can. Leaving a stone unturned on your hike through this forest of knowledge is unacceptable, because you could find something that saves your life or better yet someone else's.

Before you set off, while you are rummaging through those cabinets trying to figure out what may be needed for this voyage it's in your best interest to take the 10p's to life with you. These 10p's are like water! **<u>No one</u>** wants to find themselves stranded without water.

✓ <u>10 P's to life</u>

Prior,

Proper,

Preparation,

Prevents,

Poor,

Performance,

Poor,

Performance,

Produces,

Pain

With anything you do in life you *HAVE* to plan. Rather it be a vacation, a project, school, reaching goals, dating, no matter how big or small the task is you are trying to achieve it takes some form of planning. One of Americas founding fathers Benjamin Franklin said it best when he proclaimed, "By failing to prepare, you are preparing to fail." This one quote should be a part of the foundation that you build your life on if you desire to have success in every area of life. Along the trail you are going to blaze you will fall, you will fail, you will take a couple wrong turns, but if you hold these Ten P's close to your heart you will ALWAYS find your way.

I'm sure when you take a step back and look at the goals you desire to reach it may seem impossible to achieve them all. That is because it should seem impossible to get to that finished product. But it's not! If YOU believe YOU can, YOU will accomplish ANYTHING YOU set out to do. We can only imagine that over 2,000 years ago the architects who constructed the Great Wall of China saw this task as unreachable. Even being unsure did not stop them from laying each brick as perfectly as they could day after day. Then eventually everyone looked up and they had completed one of the great wonders of this world.

Those bricks being laid one by one represent exactly what prior proper preparation is. They show that with the consistent small efforts toward a coveted goal we make each day we eventually reach our overall goal. By making those small efforts on a regular basis we build confidence as well as knowledge. And anyone who is knowledgeable and confident in a particular area or the work they are doing will have no choice but to succeed!

Adversely, imagine if you have a test coming up or a big sporting event and you haven't studied, practiced, or even attempted to put forth any effort. How do you think you will perform? I would probably say not to well. Sometimes that one poor performance can have an effect on other areas of your life and produce a form of pain. Beyond popular belief, pain is not limited to physical, but it could manifest mentally, emotionally, or even in life problems based on decisions you made and or didn't make in the past.

Life is no different. Life in a nutshell is like a university. Whether you want to take its classes or not it will teach you something every day, and eventually life will test you over what you have learned. It is imperative to pass the test or you will have to retake each section until you get it right.

The only way you can pass is to *Be prepared!*

Tips for being prepared

- Have a plan A and a Plan B just in case plan A does not go as planned

- Be organized. Make sure everything is in order, neat, and put together in a way it can be easily found or articulated

- Write it down! This helps you remember, Who, What, When, Where, Why, and How

- Set reminders ahead of time on your phone, or on a calendar.

- Do the proper research. Make sure you are very familiar with every aspect of what you are getting ready for. *A wise person learns from those who paved the way before them.*

Now that we have the impact of being prepared down to a science, some tips on being prepared, and the 10 p's to put you ahead of the game in life, we can couple these tools with some character traits necessary for your success in anything you set out to do.

✓ *Be Fearless, Optimistic, and Hard-working*

"For God hath not given us a spirit of fear, but of power, and of love, and of sound mind."

-2nd Timothy 1:7 King James Bible-

Fear is nothing more than false evidence appearing real. Fear is not real. The only place that fear can exist is in our thoughts of the future. It is a product of our imagination, causing us to fear things that do not at present and may not ever exist. Do not misunderstand. DANGER is very real, but

FEAR is a choice. Fear can cripple your decision making, cause

anxiety or depression, and overall stagnate your growth and

forward progress if you let it.

*Choose to take a step even when you cannot see the
staircase.*

"I am not afraid of anything that can happen to me on

this earth because I know no matter what; nothing can take

my spirit from me."- Adam Brown- This is an excerpt from the

last message written by dad to the children of one of the most

heroic and fearless men to walk this earth, just in case the

worst were to happen while he was serving this country.

Adam brown was a small framed, middle child, with a heart

almost too big for his chest, from the homely town of Hot

Springs Arkansas. For the most part his early life was filled

with a few things normal to a kid in Hot Springs, like swimming

in the local swimming hole, working odd jobs as a paperboy or

at the local donut shop, and football. Oh how Mr. Brown loved

football. Coaches were afraid Adam was to skinny to take the

blunt force trauma that comes with playing varsity football,

but Adam showed them he had something more that you just

cannot coach. He had heart! He was the smallest player on the

team moving up from water boy, and never shied away from

taking on the biggest players in any drill. When he got knocked

down or plowed over almost immediately he dusted himself

off, got back up, and reset to go again. Adam would not be

stopped until he overcame any obstacle that was presented in

front of him. Even if it meant staring down the barrel of a

shotgun with smoke still in the air from the shots that had just been fired at himself, and his best friend after a fight with a group of drunk reckless drivers. He brought this same drive, perseverance, and courage with him into Navy SEAL training. Adam took those characteristics mixed with fearlessness and stared the insurgents in the Kunar Valley of Afghanistan eye to eye, in hopes of taking down their stronghold and leader. SEAL Brown took fire and had to be flown back to the base where he soon after became a casualty of war.

The most important part of this not so happy ending of a story is the mission was completed. Though it may not have been by Adam Brown, it could not have been accomplished without his willingness to be fearless, and to lay everything on the line for what he believed or to achieve the goal at hand, even if that meant death.

After the dust had settled on the battle field of the Kunar Valley John Fass a SEAL who had been with Brown on the final raid said this about his friend "Adam is the hardest man I have ever met. Over the course of his career he sustained more significant injuries than most of us combined, but he just kept on operating. He would not quit, he would not accept defeat. Not ever. Adam's devout Christian faith matched his toughness and fearlessness."

Your life and journey will mirror that of Navy SEAL Team Six Operator Adam Brown. You will get knocked down, you will fight some battles and lose, you will look at the obstacles in your life thinking that you could never overcome them, but will you get up and continue the fight even when all the odds seem stacked against you? Or will you give up, roll over, and become a casualty to your own life before achieving

anything worth mention for years to come?

What will the people close to you say about you when

it is all said and done?

What is your biggest fear/ Why can't you get rid of it:

_____

_____

_____

_____

_____

Whenever anything presents itself that makes you

uncomfortable or fearful be like Navy SEAL Team Six Operator

Adam Brown and remember the words of Franklin D.

Roosevelt during one of his Fireside Chats "The only thing to fear is fear itself." Which means things and people should <u>NOT</u>

scare you. You should only be afraid of being afraid.

<u>The Knockout Punch for FEAR:</u>

➢ Stop what you are doing and ground yourself in the

NOW, and don't be anxious of the future

➢ Take a few slow deep breaths

➢ Take control of your imagination

➢ Begin to think of a positive outcome and prepare for

that favorable future

➢ Regularly face the things that scare you taking in

consideration danger or safety

➢ Use triggers like music, or good memories to change

your mood.

➢ <u>F</u>ace, <u>E</u>verything, <u>A</u>nd, <u>R</u>ise

On the other side of the fear Libra scale is optimism. What is optimism? Optimism is looking at a more favorable side of events and simply anticipating the best possible outcome in any situation. Sir Winston Churchill says it like this, "A pessimist sees the difficulty in every opportunity; an optimist sees the opportunity in every difficulty."

What do you see?

Is the glass half-full or half empty?

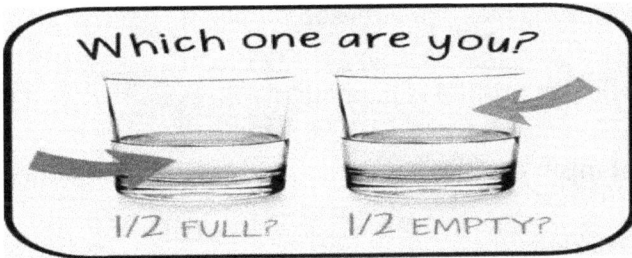

The pessimist would say half empty, but the optimist is going to say that glass is half-full!

Optimism is the balance of fear. It is having a good attitude, and having a positive outlook on life or life's situations. Optimism is being hopeful and confident of the future no matter how bad the present may look. This will be the fuel that helps you get over those speed bumps on your journey through life.

What can The "BIG O" do for you?

➢ Optimism gives you a reason for living

➢ Optimism promotes happiness

➢ Optimism enables you to put and keep your emotions in check

➢ Optimism aides in your productivity and proactivity

➢ It increases your mental, emotional, and relationship flexibility

➢ It promotes forgiveness

➢ It allows you to deal with failure constructively

What are some areas in your life you feel you could be more optimistic:

_____

_____

_____

_____

_____

_____

Optimism just like anything else in life is a choice. So, choose to look on the bright side in every situation and watch your life change for the better!

The ladder of Success to Optimism:

➤ Realize you may not be able to make a new beginning, but anyone can start today and make a new ending

➤ Look at the positives in every situation, or ways to learn from those situations

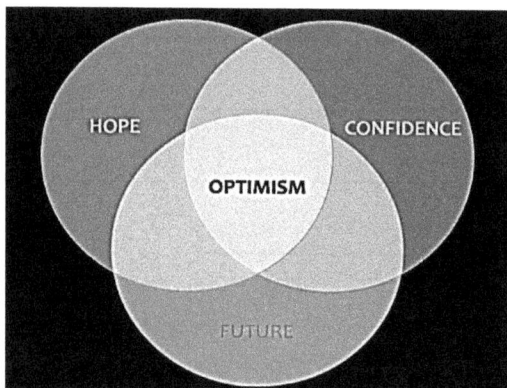

➤ Create a plan for the future, and a plan for dealing with reoccurring problems

➤ Don't make mountains out of ant beds (i.e. don't make small things into big problems.)

➢ Broaden your mental horizon by reading, introducing yourself to different cultures, or doing things out of your norm

➢ Make the necessary adjustments to ensure total confidence in everything you do.

Finally, the last strand of this not easily broken three-strand cord is none other than hard work. ***There is no substitute for hard work.*** Most people are talented, so they rely solely on the gifting they have in certain areas and procrastinate or fail to cultivate their talent through perfecting it. What they don't realize is a person who works hard beats a person with talent over time. The fact remains that anything you want to know or do in life can be learned. If you work hard enough at it, and dedicate enough time to it you can become an expert, and write your own checks.

The late 1980's were a time where America was changing for the better. This period marked a peak of freedom of speech being practiced and accepted from all walks of life in The United States. An eighteen-year-old kid from Philadelphia saw this as a perfect opportunity to speak about a group of individuals he felt stifled his independence and creativity... *Parents*! With a close friend, he wrote and made a song expressing exactly how he felt that rose to the top of the charts. That fame quickly faded and to him his life felt idled and unfulfilling.

At the doldrums of his success, a popular television company by the name of NBC gave him a call with an idea for a show about his life. He agreed. Not knowing much about television his first season was a disaster. His performances were often washed out or drab compared to his more seasoned counter parts. Also, he could often be seen on camera mouthing the parts of the other characters to insure he presented his line on time. With the pressure to perform on his shoulders, his confidence was at an all- time low. On top of all of that, the producers threatened to cancel the show.

Knowing this, that kid from Philly mustered up the only thing he did have which was his work ethic and gave 110%, putting in countless hours preparing.

On the next season, he along with everyone else involved created an experience that transcended barriers. The show is "The Fresh Prince of Bel-Air." The actor is Will Smith who is a household name even today. Why, can be summed up in one quote from the actor in one of his many interviews, "You may have more talent than me, or be more skilled than me, but if we get on a treadmill together either you're getting off first or I'm going to die on that treadmill. It's as simple as that!"

He and all the other successful people possess a special skill that takes time to be able to master. That skill is the art of being able to summon that extra person inside of you. Because no matter how hard you work, how hard you train, or how disciplined you are there will always be someone inside of you who is more hardworking, that trains harder, and is more disciplined. If you can become best friends with that person there are no limits to where you can go.

But how do I even set up a meeting with this person?

The answer is P.U.S.H. Persevere Until Something Happens. Don't quit, Don't give up, Don't be afraid to fail, just keeping pushing, and persevere through any obstacle that comes in your way. When your mind is telling you that you can't go any further, *KEEP GOING!* That inner person will meet you right there on the track and carry you past the finish line. Practicing this consistently will melt away any barriers you have placed on yourself. Making you more confident in yourself.

Vince Lombardi, 6-time NFL champion and arguably the greatest American football coach to grace the earth exclaimed at the beginning of his team's championship seasons that,

"The price of success is hard work, dedication to the job at hand, and the determination that whether we win or lose we have applied the best of ourselves to the task at hand."

I'm sure on Michael Jordan's quest for greatness he embodied this mantra after he was cut from his high school team! But, he was optimistic of his future, developed fearlessness of failure, and then worked tirelessly towards being **HIS** best. Eventually all those people who were more talented than him in high school were sitting in the audience as spectators when he was enshrined into The National Basketball Association's Hall of Fame. His drive teaches us not to despise our humble beginnings, everything that YOU go through is growing YOU and preparing YOU for YOUR future, and most importantly, ***failure is not final!***

Thomas Edison failed over 1,000 times in a row before he got it right with the lightbulb. Failure is just a reminder of what didn't work, and what can be improved.

This hard work concept is not magic. The only real trick to working hard is to consistently put forth a directed effort toward that which you wish to achieve. When you find yourself unmotivated to P.U.S.H use this small reminder to get you over that hump.

JUST DO IT ALREADY!

"If every decision and choice you make is just about you. At a certain point you will hit something that's a lot tougher than you, and it's going to make you quit because you don't have a driving force for why you do what you do." - Inky Johnson-

> *Focus on your why and your who.*

What motivates you:

_____

_____

_____

Who motivates you:

_____

_____

_____

> ➤ *Create small, easily achievable goals*

What is a big goal that you have:

_____

_____

_____

What small steps can you take each day to reach that goal:

_____

_____

_____

_____

➢ *Change viewing what YOU have to do as hard work, to just a small hurdle YOU have to jump over to get where you want to go.*

➢ *Control what you can and make your best out of the rest.*

➢ *Set a time line and deadline to achieve these goals*

➢ *Use the chain method:*

The chain method is taking a big calendar and a bright colored marker. Place that calendar in an area you see it easily and often. Make a big X on the days when you put forth any effort toward your goal. Eventually you will develop a chain of X's

that mentally you will not want to break.

➢ Celebrate YOUR wins and YOUR small victories.

"Hard work beats talent when talent fails to work hard."-

Kevin Durant-

✓ <u>Your GPA is A MAJOR KEY!</u>

"I just knew what I wanted to be since third grade. And I

always did well in school. I was the type to get good grades; I

never really got below C's or nothing like that. I always kept

it A-B." -Big Sean-

What does GPA stand for:

_____

What is your current GPA:_____

What is your target GPA:_____

The better YOUR GPA the easier it is for YOU, as simple as

that.

Calculating your GPA is not rocket science, but it is a necessary tool you as a student should possess. Because it is made up of all your grades, your GPA is one of the most important things for college admission. It is a good indicator to your college of choice of your intelligence, work ethic, perseverance, and willingness when given a task to perform well at it.

How to Calculate Your GPA:

1. Look at your grades and give them a numerical value

    based on a 4.0 scale. Follow the table given.

Grade Equivalent Table for 4.0 scale:

Letter Grade	Numerical Equivalent
A	4.0
B	3.0
C	2.0
D	1.0
F	0.0

2. Add all of the numeric decimal grades together to

    create a sum.

Life hack 101: The Ultimate Guide to College Success

Example:

A +A +C+B +B+A

Is equivalent to...

4.0+4.0+2.0+3.0+3.0+4.0 = **(20.0)**

3. Take this sum and divide it by the total number of
   classes or grades.

Example:

Our sum of (20.0) / the 6 classes used to calculate that sum =

3.33 (Your GPA)

Let's try it:

Jordan gets his report card and finds out he has 3A's, 4B's, and 1C. Based on the grades given what is his current GPA?

3(___) +4(___) +1(___) =_____

Sum of decimal equivalents (_____) / Number of classes taken (___) = _____(Jordan's Current GPA)

Use this method to calculate your own GPA.

Now that we know how to calculate our GPA's let's take a look at how easily a few bad grades can affect your GPA.

Imagine:

Taylor, a student in your class is extremely smart. They fall asleep in class, but always seem to make a 100 on every test. They say to themselves "It's too easy. Why should I do homework when I know I'm going to ace every test?"

A table outlining Taylor's class grades can be found below.

Test #1	**100**
Test #2	**95**
Quiz #1	**90**
Quiz#2	**87**
Homework #1	**0**
Homework #2	**0**
Homework #3	**0**

Let's calculate Taylor's grade

Assuming all of the grades in this class hold the same weight

Taylor's average would be

(Sum of all grades) / (# of grades used) = Her class average

(___) / (___) = **53.1%**

This is why your best effort and all grades are important.

If Taylor turned in all of her homework and made at

least 50% on each one, her average would increase to 74.6%

for the class. That is a difference of almost 22%. This means a

jump of 2 letter grades and huge boost to her GPA.

"The only place success comes before work is in the

dictionary." –Vince Lombardi-

Beyond popular belief your GPA counts and is being

calculated as soon as you walk through those high school

doors. So take all of your classes seriously and aim to perform

at your best. Do you really want to be the person who makes

it all the way to senior year and has trouble graduating or

getting into their favorite college because they did not take

their grades seriously from the beginning?

The Rocket Booster's to help your GPA soar

1. Take electives or extra credit courses that come easy to you.

Most times, there are up to four or five classes that you

have to take that will act as your electives. Do your best to not

put extra stress on yourself by choosing something

challenging. Opt out for something that you enjoy, are good

at, or already know a little about and plan on learning more after you graduate. The fact that you like the subject will give you that extra push to excel in it.

Even during your senior year, you may have an option to take a couple periods off. If you do not have a job or something more productive to do take a couple more classes you know you can make a high grade in and pad your GPA just a little bit more.

2. Take Advanced Placement Classes

If you excel in a certain subject like Math, English, Science, History, etc. try to get in an advanced placement or accelerated version of that course if possible. Most people do not realize AP classes raise your GPA higher than a traditional version of the same class.

So if any subject comes easy to you, use that to your advantage **_now_** to put yourself in a better position later. A recent study found that the percentage for students that graduate college in five years or less after taking AP courses improves by up to 50%!

3. Make Straight A's

There is no better way to help ensure you have a prime GPA than to **MAKE GOOD GRADES**. Your best bet is to not even leave it up to chance by striving for straight A's. Yes, it may take more work, you will have to sacrifice more, and maybe even get more help, but it will be worth it in the end. Work hard now and make your future a whole lot easier. *YOU CAN DO IT! PUT YOUR BRAIN TO IT!* It's not impossible. The word itself screams to you *I'M... POSSIBLE!* Don't be afraid to get help. If you need help *GET HELP*, that goes for anything in life especially with school. Don't let the problem grow. It will only get worse as time ticks, and eventually it may even be too late to fix.

✓ *Know the School Counselor*

Every school has a counselor or person who is in charge of keeping up with GPA's, class rankings, and all things college. These people are there to help guide you along your plan. Make sure you are on a first name basis with these people. The reason being is not only do your counselors hold valuable information for your future, but life after grade school is not always what you know, but it is who you know.

Stop by the counselor's office every now and ask about any progress that has been made, any opportunities for involvement, and especially to keep up with your grade point average and class ranking. It's YOUR responsibility to stay on top of these things. **Not your parents, or the schools.** It is very possible for an error to occur in any one of these areas. This error could start a snowball effect that will roll onto your future and crush any dreams you may have had.

✓ *Ask The Right Questions*

"Judge a person by his questions rather than their answers."
-Voltaire-

You should ALWAYS ask questions! There should be no fear in not knowing something because 9 times out of 10 someone else has the same question and is afraid to ask it too.

But don't let this be an excuse to ask a rhetorical question or not have a clear concise point you want to make. Do your research ahead of time then ask for clarity, or knowledge that you could not find on your own.

Listed are some of the questions you should ask before you graduate.

To yourself:

1. What do I want to achieve and be remembered for while I'm here?

2. What is my plan after I leave here?

3. What can I do now to help me reach my future goals?

4. Am I doing MY very best in everything I attempt?

5. What areas could I use improvement?

To the counselor:

1. What can I do now to prepare for college?

2. What is my GPA (grade point average)?

3. What is my class ranking?

4. How is my GPA and class ranking calculated?

5. What is the date for the final update of our GPA and class ranking before we graduate?

6. What test do I need to take in preparation for college?

7. How can I raise my GPA?

8. What volunteer opportunities are available?

9. When are college application, scholarship, and financial aid deadlines?

10. What organizations are offered that I can get involved in to better prepare me for what I want to do in college?

11. Am I on the right track?

12. Are there any classes I can take that are not required but will aid me in my college pursuit?

These are some basic questions to ask yourself as well as your counselor. You can always add to this list if the need arises. One thing you should remember when dealing with your counselor is to always be respectful as well as grateful. Most grade school counselors go above and beyond what they are required to do to help your life be just a little bit easier. So make an effort to thank them. In addition, always do what you can to be prepared for your encounters with your counselor or advisor.

Before we go further, take a moment to process all the wonderful tools you have gained thus far, and can use starting today to give you an extra boost above your competition as it relates to being prepared for scholastic success.

Now, while you are in this sensible state have you ever asked yourself how can I make a difference, or save the world? Many people struggle with this question day in and day out causing them to feel regretful, and most times not even try to accomplish any effort toward the betterment of humanity. It may be because they think saving the world is a task far too colossal for any one man or woman to undertake. What if I told you that is not true? What if I told you right now there is something you can do to change the world?

Well there is!

✓ *Go the Extra Mile... Volunteer*

"Service to others is the rent you pay for your room here on earth!" -Muhammad Ali-

Volunteering is more than spending a couple hours doing something you probably would never have thought you would do. It is the icing on the cake. It is a gateway for you to become well rounded, and selfless. The short amount of time you spend or that small exhibit of care and kindness could mean the world to someone. It is your duty to give back to others especially if you have been blessed enough to be in a position to do so. A world-renowned author and motivational speaker by the name of Zig Ziglar once said in one of his thousands of speeches across the globe that "You will get what you want in life, if you help enough other people get what they want."

By giving of your time and efforts, not only are you building yourself up and helping others, but you are also making yourself stand out above the crowd. You are separating yourself from the pack and rising to the top of that success ladder.

As it relates to your future scholastic endeavors, some colleges strongly recommend volunteer hours. To them it shows you have character, you are selfless, you hold highly doing whatever it takes to better your community, and you have a sense of responsibility. Many colleges use volunteering as a way to set student applications apart. Some colleges even have scholarships solely based on amount of volunteer participation. The best mindset to have towards service is not to think less of yourself, but think of yourself less!

Volunteering is not rocket science or trying to solve the major problems of the world. You can do almost anything and have an impact.

Some examples could include:

A local food bank

A local animal shelter

The Boys and Girls Club or Y.M.C.A

Picking up trash around your neighborhood

Helping with school events

Helping a local church or non-profit

Goodwill Stores

Some grocery chains

Donating can goods or clothes

Feeding the homeless, especially during holidays

The opportunities are endless!

The number of volunteer hours you should aim for each year starting freshman year in high school is 20-30 hours. It may seem like a lot at first but like stated earlier knock it out in small spurts throughout the year. The more volunteer hours you have the better you look on paper and the closer you put yourself to the top when being considered for college or even jobs. Anything from 50 hours to 200 hours will help you stand out, but remember the more hours you have the better.

To help you keep track of your progress draw a thermometer on a white piece of paper, draw numbers in increments of 5 representing a build up to your hourly goal, color in your thermometer with your favorite color until you reach your goal, then celebrate.

I understand it may be hard to find time to volunteer with your busy schedule. It doesn't have to be. In one of Confucius many groundbreaking quotes he stated that "When it is obvious that the goals cannot be reached, don't adjust the goals, adjust the action steps." Use Confucius' quote as the foundation in which you use to achieve any goal you set.

All it takes is one hour per week:

1hr /wk. for a year = 52hrs

3hrs/wk. for a year = 156hrs

1hr/day after school for half a year = roughly 80hrs by winter break

You can do almost anything and gain volunteer hours. Check with the school counselors for school wide opportunities. Always make sure you keep a detailed log of your volunteering with signatures from appropriate leadership.

Giving of your time, energy, and belongings to others has its benefits as well.

➢ Volunteering connects you to others

➢ Volunteering provides a sense of purpose

➢ Volunteering gives you a better appreciation for your life

➢ Volunteering helps counteract depression, anger, anxiety, and stress

➢ Volunteering can teach you valuable skills

➢ Volunteering can advance or improve your career

➢ Volunteering can set you apart in the college application process

"The best way to find yourself is to lose yourself in the service of others." –Mahatma Gandhi-

Even after you have done all of this and excelled at each level there is one singular thing that can hold you back when initially trying to cross over into being a successful college student. That one concept is standardized test. Nobody likes them but they are highly effective at gauging on a wide spectrum a student's abilities to learn, think critically, and retain valuable information. Here I have laid out some sure fire ways to put you in the best position to perform YOUR best on any test but more importantly the SAT and ACT!

✓ *Acing The Big Test*

"Believe you can and you're halfway there"

―Theodore Roosevelt-

Nothing looks better on a college application than a high grade point average AND great tests scores. Standardized testing can be a pain, and may not always be fair but it is necessary especially for your scholastic success.

See how you measure up below:

School	**New SAT Comp**	**New ACT Comp**
UT Austin	1220-1450	25-31
Harvard Univ.	**1480-1600**	**32-35**
Alabama	1070-1310	22-31
Washington St.	**990-1200**	**19-26**

This chart represents what most of the freshman that currently attend those schools scored on their standardized test. If you don't quite measure up just yet that is fine, there is still time for improvement. To get where you want to be you must first be totally honest with where you are.

What is your highest cumulative SAT score: _____

What is your highest cumulative ACT score: _____

What are the ACT/SAT score requirements to get into your top schools:

_____

_____

_____

All colleges when deciding your future at their campus look at two major tests. These are the ACT and the SAT. I'm sure you have heard of them both. It is imperative that you do well on at least one of these tests. A passing score that will get you into most 4 year universities is a 1000 on the new SAT scoring out of 1600, and a 19 on the ACT out of 36. These two scores are average as it relates to the test. Even if you find yourself close to this line ***DON'T PANIC***. You can still have future success in college and life. However, keep in mind most colleges give scholarships to incoming freshman based on how they perform on either of these standardized testing

measurements.

Your test scores accompanied with your GPA is a very important aspect in your immediate success after high school.

If you haven't noticed already, a common theme in this

book for your success in any aspect of life is preparation. Now

that you know where you are and where you need to go let's

focus in on how to get there.

How to get that Ace in the Hole

1. **Be aware of what you need to score to excel at your**

choice school. Having a goal or a vision is a big factor in

reaching it. Most people don't fail because they aim to high and miss, but because they aim to low and hit the mark every

time.

2. **AIM HIGH!** Shoot for the stars and perfection. Even if you

miss you will find yourself somewhere in the clouds. (ACT=36,

SAT=1600)

Believe you can do anything you set your mind to, and tell

yourself you can every single day.

Repeat 18 Times: "I can do ANYTHING I set my mind to do!"

3. **Be Prepared**

- Bring the necessary tools i.e. (a few #2 pencils, a

  scientific calculator with fresh batteries, identification,

water and a snack if possible, and don't forget your

confidence.)

- Get a good night's rest. (at least 8 hours undisturbed)

4. *STUDY! STUDY! STUDY!*

- There is nothing new on this test. Many of the practice

  test or prep courses have almost identical questions to

  the ones that will be presented on testing day. Try to be

  as familiar as possible with these questions.

- There are many prep courses to help you succeed in

this area. The programs I have found to be most effective

are the ones offered by the actual ACT and SAT website.

They are around $50, which is a fraction of the price you

would pay for a tutor. There are also a number of previous

test you can use *FOR FREE*!

Sample Testing Questions:

Part 1: English

DIRECTIONS: In the paragraph that follows, certain words and phrases are underlined and numbered. Following that paragraph, you will find alternatives for the underlined parts. You are to choose the answer choice that best expresses the idea, makes the statement appropriate for standard written English, or is worded more consistently with the style and tone of the passage as a whole. If you think the original version is best, choose 'NO CHANGE'

The Triangular Snowflake

Snowflakes *form from tiny water droplets,* (1) following a specific process of chemical bonding as they freeze, which results in a six-figured figure. The rare

"triangular" snowflake, *similarly,(2)* confounded scientist for

years because it apparently defied the basic laws of

chemistry. [A] The seemingly triangular shape of those

snowflakes suggest *that forming* (3) through a different

process of chemical bonding. [B] By re-creating snowflake

formation, *a discovery has revealed to scientist Kenneth*

Libbrecht and Hannah Arnold the cause of this apparent

variation.(4)

1. **A.** NO CHANGE
   B. form, from tiny, water droplets
   C. form from tiny, water, droplets
   D. form, from tiny water droplets

2. **F.** NO CHANGE
   G. for example,
   H. additionally,
   J. however,

3. **A.** NO CHANGE
   B. the manner in which formation
   C. which had formed
   D. that they form

4. **F.** NO CHANGE
   G. the discovery of the cause of this apparent variation has been made by scientists Kenneth Libbrecht and Hannah Arnold.
   H. scientist Kenneth Libbrecht and Hannah Arnold have discovered the cause of this apparent variation.
   J. the cause of this apparent variation has been discovered by scientists Kenneth Libbrecht and Hannah Arnold.

Tip: *Always use process of elimination. You can eliminate usually one or two answers right away!*

Part 2: Mathematics

Directions: Solve each problem, choose the correct answer, and then fill in the corresponding oval on your answer document. You are permitted to use a calculator on this test.

The blood types of 150 people were determined for a study as shown in the figure below.

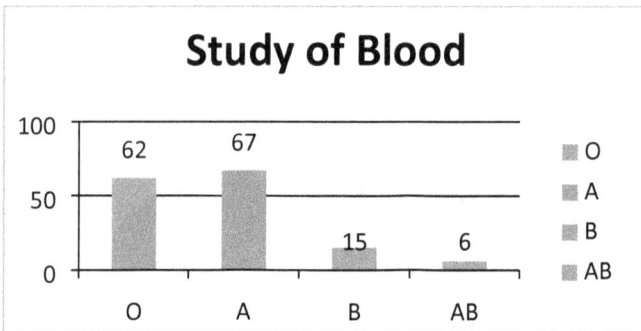

1. If one person from this study is randomly selected what is the probability that this person would have either type A or type AB blood?
   A. 62/150
   B. 66/150
   C. 68/150
   D. 73/150
   E. 84/150

2. The monthly fees for single rooms at 5 colleges are $370, $310, $380, $340, and $310 respectively. What is the mean of these monthly fees?
    F. $310
    G. $340
    H. $342
    J. $350
    K. $380

3. Given $F=cd^3$, F=450, and d=10 what is c?

    A. 0.45 B. 4.5 C. 15 D. 45 E. 150

Answers

Sample 1:1 A

Sample 1:2 J

Sample 1:3 D

Sample 1:4 H

Sample 2:1 D

Sample 2:2 H

Sample 2:3 A

How did you measure up?

It's ok if you didn't do too hot on these practice

questions. Use this as a litmus test to decide if you could use a

little more work. Even if you did do well with these practice

questions you can never be too prepared. So find practice test

that are free to help perfect those test taking skills.

5. **Remember the test is timed**! So prepare for it by timing

yourself during your study sessions and practice runs. By doing

this you are seeing what areas will take you more time and

more focus during the real test. This technique is also training

you for the pace of the test. I'm almost certain during the

actual exam it will feel like time is moving a lot faster.

6. **Be there on time.** Most times if you are late you will be turned away at the door. Remember if you are on time you are late, if you are early you are on time. Give yourself enough time not to have to rush, or be in a frantic state of mind. Take the necessary measures to ensure you stay calm, cool, and collected. ***WOOSAH!!!***

7. **If at first you don't succeed try try again.**

- There is no limit to how many times you can take these tests. Take them as many times as you need to get your best score. Start early; try to take the real test before senior year or even junior year so you don't have to rush come crunch time.

8. **Eat a healthy breakfast**. Your brain is a muscle that needs fuel. Make sure you put premium gasoline in on this day. *NO JUNK FOOD* high in sugar. Reach for fruits and berries, or whole grains. *DRINK WATER!*

Whew! Wipe your forehead and stand a little taller because you have passed with flying colors. By using that blueprint there is nothing that can hold you back from making a perfect score on both the SAT and ACT.

Now we have gotten all of the particulars out the way and shouldn't be worrying about our grades or our test scores we can continue to move forward on our quest confidently.

✓ <u>College Applications</u>

"Twenty years from now, you will be more disappointed by the things you didn't do than by the ones you did do. So, throw off the bowlines. Sail away from the safe harbor. Catch the trade winds in your sails. Explore, Dream, Discover." –Mark Twain-

Finally, you have reached the fun part. This is the part where all that prior preparation and those countless hours of studying, volunteering, and taking the essential steps needed to make exceptional grades come into play. Filling out college applications can be overwhelming. But you have picked up all the necessary things along the way to help you do this. These days there is a Life Hack for everything. Try this Life Hack for college applications and give yourself a little more peace as you ascend to the summit of this mountain

YOUR Top 5 college choices:

1. _____

2. _____

3. _____

4. _____

5. _____

Now that you have a starting point and a direction in which to aim your arrow, we can focus on how to make sure that arrow hits the right bull's-eye.

I. *Be aware of approaching deadlines*

Most colleges have application deadlines that end the year prior to your graduation date, or the months before you actually graduate. So always make sure you are aware of any approaching deadlines and you have fulfilled all the requirements of that application before the deadline. Two very important national deadline ranges to keep in mind are the early application deadline usually ranges from Nov. 1-Nov. 15, and the regular deadline is usually from January 1st – February 1st. The earlier you get your application in the better it is for YOU!

II. __Work smarter not harder__

There are a few websites where you can apply to multiple schools at the same time like www.Commonapp.org,www.Universalcollegeapp.com, www.ApplyTexas.org , and many more.

Utilize these websites especially for the schools that do not have an application fee associated with the process. The most important thing to consider when applying to colleges is

picking the school that best fits your needs and desires.

III. *Have a few tricks up your sleeve*

Almost all college applications have an associated processing

fee. Always keep this in mind when choosing which schools to apply

to first. BUT there are ways that those fees can be waived, or paid

later. Make sure you read everything at the end of the application

and see if there is a fee waiver you qualify for. Also, contact that

school and ask if you can have the fees waived for a certain

period of time or even indefinitely.

You never know what you can get just by asking for it.

Now, imagine if you want to be a doctor or study any

profession at one of the top schools in the nation, but you do not meet the requirements to get into that particular program at this moment. Before you get sad, there is a back door that you may be able to walk through. Most if not all schools offer a general application or a general studies application. The qualifications for these types of applications are usually much lower and easier to be accepted into. Once your application is approved you can always change your major and earn acceptance into your college of choice after your first semester much easier. Now always do your due diligence in researching if the school you plan on attending binds you to a certain major. Some schools like University of Texas have become aware of this simple hack and in turn put in place the necessary measures in attempt to discourage this methodology.

> **Remember:** Have a secondary plan. Never forget that by networking with the right people, and proving yourself through grades and community/campus involvement your 1st year in college you may be able to earn acceptance into your desired field of study!

IV. *Consider every possible avenue*

Make sure you have an idea of what you want to study in college or what career path you want to travel when starting the application process. Even if it is not concrete or you feel you may want to change it at least have a direction in which to aim your arrow.

Sometimes instead of going to a 4-year university and creating a ton of unnecessary debt, you can opt out for a technical or community college. These schools are specialized and more economic as it relates to cost. They tend to cut straight to the point instead of forcing you to take a few classes that don't have much to do with your career goals.

This is the most important line of the College application section. ***<u>Whoever gives you the most money is who you want to take seriously because they already have showed you that they value you and take you seriously.</u>*** A wise man by the name of Matthew said this "For where your treasure is, there your heart will also be," and I believe that statement to be true.

V. <u>Early Decision vs. Early Admittance(Action)</u>

A wide spread confusion among high school students who have started the application process for college is the early decision vs. early admittance dilemma. Both commitments are roughly identical with the exception that early decision actually binds you to attend that particular college. This means you may **_NOT_** apply to or attend any other college if you have accepted a certain university's early decision offer. Another plan of action in addition to ED or EA to consider when shuffling through the application process is the single-choice early action, under which applicants may not apply ED or EA to any other college.

The Early Bird Gets The Worm (Priority Apps.)

Applying to an ED or EA plan is most appropriate for a student who:

- Has researched all possible college options
- Is 100% sure that the college is their first choice
- Has found a college that matches their needs personally, and scholastically
- Meets or exceeds the admissions requirements at the college for SAT/ACT scores, GPA, and class rank.

Applying to an ED or EA plan is not appropriate for a student who:

- Has not thoroughly researched all possible college options
- Is applying early just to avoid the strenuous application process
- Is not without a doubt committed to attending that college.
- Needs a strong senior fall semester to bring grades up

VI.   <u>Super-scoring</u>

Over the years, many colleges have taken into consideration the all too common flaw of human error. Some of them have even gone as far as making exceptions that take into account human error and make the application process a little fairer. One of the ways institutions have done this is by implementing super-scoring into their application decision process. This is nothing more than taking the best attempt of the applicant on a certain standardized test. For instance, if you take the SAT two times the person reviewing applications

will take your best scores from each attempt.

On the following page is an example of one student's

grades on the SAT that they have sent to their college

admissions office.

Figure 1:	1st attempt	2nd attempt
Reading/ Writing	450	**_550_**
Math	**_600_**	425

As we see in **Figure 1** the highlighted and underlined scores would be the ones the college admissions office accepts even though they were from different attempts on the same test. Keep in mind that some schools use the super-scoring method, but others like Howard University and Texas A&M strictly go by the first set of scores or application that is received from the prospective student.

TIP: If you don't know or you can't find out whether your school accepts multiple applications, or super-scoring assume the latter and put your best attempt forward from the beginning!

✓ *Show Me The Money (Financial Aid Guide)*

$12,000 was the average cost for college tuition and board in the year 2000 at the beginning of the 21st century. Only 16 years later that cost has skyrocketed to roughly $20,000 as stated on ***collegeboard.com***. This trend will more than likely continue in the coming years so financial aid will begin to be more and more important. With that being said, there are many types of aid that can pay for school. However, before you attempt to utilize any of them you **must** first fill out the **F**ree **A**pplication for **F**ederal **S**tudent **A**id or FAFSA. This can be found here at ***fafsa.ed.gov.*** Most colleges require you to fill this out first before you can be considered for any type of aid. Another application to consider is the *College Scholarship Service*. Not many schools use this application, but it could be mandatory for the school you plan to attend. Most private institutions that accept early admissions use this to determine possible aid students could be awarded for a desired year. Be cautious that there is a cost associated with this method, but there are always fee waivers.

To increase your chances for financial aid remember the early bird gets the worm and do your best to apply by the earliest deadline at ***Fafsa.ed.gov.***

Before you start the FAFSA,

here are the documents you'll need to have on hand. If you're a dependent student, you'll need all of these from your parents as well:

Your Social Security number.

Your driver's license number, if you have one.

Your alien registration number if you're not a U.S. citizen.

Records of investments, including stocks and bonds and real estate (not including the home you live in), and business and farm assets.

A Federal Student Aid PIN to sign electronically. (You can get one at www.pin.ed.gov.)

Bank statements, savings and checking account balances.

Records of untaxed income, including child support, interest income and veterans non-education benefits.

Federal tax, including W-2s.

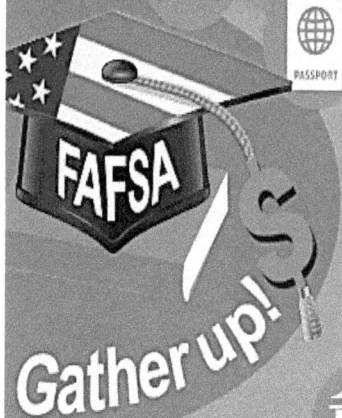

Gather up!

FAFSA CHECKLIST

Step 1

Get a PIN

Must have Soical Security Number

Apply at www.pin.ed.gov

Step 2

Fill out the FAFSA

Go to www.fafsa.gov

Need your family's tax info

Sign with PIN

Send it in ASAP

It's free! (beware of scam websites)

Step 3

FAFSA Processing

Dept of Ed processes FAFSA and
sends to colleges of your choice

Sudent Aid Report (SAR)

Expected Family Contribution (EFC)

You'll recieve these numbers in
an e-mail.

Step 4

How much did I get?

School will determine how much you get based on EFC

Compare financial packages from each school and
choose which one works best for you

Respond to the finanical aid offer from the college
you chose

For more information visit: studentaid.ed.gov

There are a few common misconceptions people have about the FAFSA you may hear, but should pay no attention to. These include:

1. Only low-income families qualify for financial aid.

2. Setting up a college fund in your child's name is the best way to save for college.

3. Colleges require you to pay FAFSA's expected family contribution.

4. It costs money to file your FAFSA form.

5. You can only apply for financial aid your senior year of high school.

"We believe, that is, you and I, that education is not an expense. We believe it is an investment."

- Lyndon B. Johnson-

CSS Profile:

Most of the information in the CSS Profile section came directly from http://css.collegeboard.org/

Who Must Submit

Not all colleges and scholarship programs require the PROFILE application. Check with the ones you're interested in to see if they require it.

When to Register and Submit

You should register at CSS/Financial Aid PROFILE at least two weeks before the earliest college/ scholarship application priority date you need to meet. This date is the college or program's deadline for submitting a completed PROFILE application.

Once you register, you can complete the PROFILE application right away or save your data and return to it later. Just be sure to complete and submit the application by the deadlines your colleges or scholarship programs specify.

How Much It Costs

Sending your PROFILE report to one college or scholarship program costs $25. Additional reports are $16 each. Domestic students who are completing PROFILE for the first time and who used an SAT fee waiver can receive up to eight PROFILE fee waivers. To qualify, students must log in to PROFILE using the same account used for the SAT. Students who did not use an SAT fee waiver may still qualify for a PROFILE fee waiver based on income.

The most common types of financial aid include:

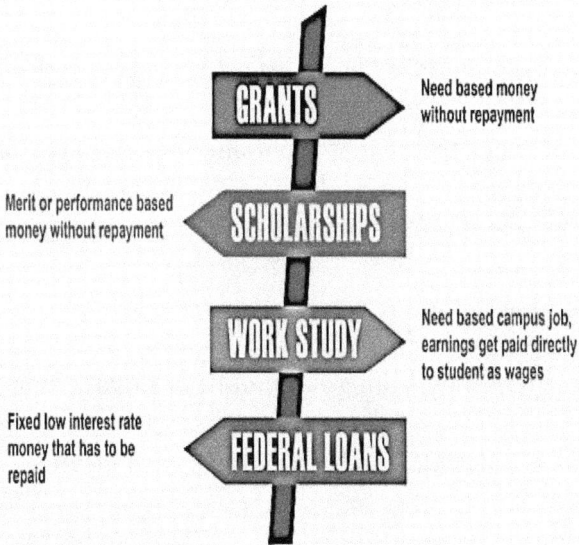

Need based money
without repayment

GRANTS

Merit or performance based
money without repayment

SCHOLARSHIPS

WORK STUDY

Need based campus job,
earnings get paid directly
to student as wages

Fixed low interest rate
money that has to be
repaid

FEDERAL LOANS

1. *Grants-* Money given by the government that IS NOT

   required to be paid back

A. A Common Grant to search for is the Pell Grant which

   is awarded by need based on the amount of money

   you and your parents made the previous year

B. If you or a parent served this country in any branch of national defense, you should qualify for The Hazelwood Grant, which **pays for everything!**

C. Also, check to see if affluent alumnae donated to your college in the form of a program or grant. Grants are the type of money you want to have for college.

2. *Loans-* Money from government or private lenders that IS REQUIRED to be paid back **with interest**

A. Common Loans include the *Subsidized loans* that start gaining interest after you graduate or have been out of school for more than 6 months to a year.

B. *Unsubsidized loans* which start gaining interest while you are still in school

C. *Always read the fine print on EVERYTHING. Find out the best plan possible for you including repayment.*

D. _Parent Plus Loan_ If you need more money your parents can apply for a lower interest loan which helps you whether they qualify or not

While you are in school these loans can help build your credit

E. If you do have to take out loans that are not required to be paid back until you graduate, they can help. While you are enrolled in school it looks to the lender as if you are making regular on time payments back towards that loan. This could help you build up your credit for the future.

F. However, even though loans have a bright side they should not be your first choice or primary method of financial aid. The reason is that they <u>DO</u> have to be paid back, and the payback amount is much more than

the amount you borrowed.

G. ***Be Aware of private loan lenders.*** These types of

lenders usually have high interest rates that would

cause you to pay back often 3 times more than you

actually borrowed. They are not always set up to

benefit students like Sallie Mae's un-sub and sub loans.

Let's Play A Game (Loans Will Rob You):

Direct Subsidized Loans   ***Undergraduate***

3.76%

Direct Unsubsidized Loans   ***Undergraduate***
3.76%

Direct Unsubsidized Loans   ***Graduate or Professional***
5.31%

The amount of interest that accrues (accumulates) on your

loan from month to month is determined by a simple daily

interest formula. This formula consists of multiplying your

loan balance by the number of days since the last payment times the interest rate factor.

Simple daily interest formula:

(Outstanding principal balance)
x (number of days since last payment)
x (interest rate factor)
= interest amount

Let's Say:

Your principle balance on your loan is $5,000 and you are 30 days late with an interest rate that is 3.76% for your Direct Subsidized Loan. What would your interest amount be that is added to your principle balance?

($5,000) x (30) x (.0376) = $5,640 (interest amount)

Now it is easy to see why most people never pay off their college loans, or spend their whole life trying to pay back a small loan they took out in college. One rule of thumb here is to never take more than you need.

When it comes to loans never take more than you need!

3. <u>*Scholarships-*</u> are money awarded for merit that has certain qualifications and rules, but is not required to be paid back under most circumstances

A. *Scholly:* is an app that can be downloaded on a smart phone that gives you access to any and every scholarship you could qualify for in the world.

B. A website for the top ten scholarship resource sites is as follows

http://college.usatoday.com/2012/01/30/the-10-best-sites-to-look-for-scholarships/

C. Some of the best ones are www.Zinch.com, www.Scholarships.com, www.fastweb.com, **and** www.nextstudent.com

D. Always check your college of choices scholarships and aid they may have available exclusively for incoming freshman. Be aware of their exclusive deadlines.

E. Check your church or local businesses and organizations. Sometimes they have extra money they can give away.

F. There is a scholarship for graduating high school early. If this case applies to you use it to your advantage.

G. As stated by Cecillia Barr in her research on Debt.org an estimated $46 Billion in scholarships and grants is awarded each year. That's billion with a "B"! But even though $46 Billion dollars is awarded according to a recent study by Nerd Scholar, the higher education

team at Nerd Wallet high school seniors left more than

$2.9 Billion in unused free money on the table in 2014.

There's a scholarship for that:

- ❖ *Prom Guide's Cutest Couple Contest $1000*

- ❖ *Create-A-Greeting Card Scholarship Contest $10,000*

- ❖ *Doodle for Google $30,000*

- ❖ *Little people of America Scholarship $1,000*

- ❖ *Scholarship Red for natural Red-heads $500*

- ❖ *Tall Club for women at least 5'10 and men at least 6'2*

  $1,000

- ❖ *Zombie Apocalypse Scholarship $2,000*

- ❖ *Pokémon World Championship Scholarship $500-*

  $10,000

VII. <u>*Set application goals for yourself. "You should want*</u>

<u>*to have a certain number of applications done by a*</u>

<u>*certain time."*</u>

Finally, we are almost done with this college

application business. However, what is this? There's

more?!?

✓ <u>*Application prompts and essay question*</u>

The essay portion is the best part of the whole process.

It is your chance to emerge from the black and white

particulars of application jargon to making a personal and

hopefully moving connection with your future Alma Mater.

This is the most personal part that can make or break

the outstanding college application we have fostered thus far.

You will be given a chance to tell your unique story in hopes of

capturing the reader's attention in a way that moves the

chords of their emotions. At the end of almost all college

applications, there is a section that asks a more personal

question from the others you have already answered during

the application process. Here you must relate this question to

a one of a kind instance in your own life. To make it even more

difficult there is a time limit or word count limit depending on

the school. Usually these prompts only allow you 500 words or

less. So to help you succeed in this area be familiar with those prompts and have sample answers that are within the set

parameters.

USE SPILL CHEEK → USE SPELL CHECK

Make sure to practice proper grammar and or

punctuation. This very important aspect could possibly

disqualify you if you are not careful even though you may be

the best candidate. Use this rule when filling out any type of

application.

Imagine if you were an employer or the person in

charge of reviewing applicants. While you were going through

your stack, you find an application riddled with grammatical

and spelling errors. If that was me sitting behind that desk I

would slide that application to my dubious stack of *NOT*

GOING TO HIRE, or even the trash can. Many people

unknowingly disqualify themselves this way before the race

even starts! A great help is to type your answers into

Microsoft Word, then copy and paste them as the need arises.

Some recent sample essay prompts from

*www.commonapp.org**include:*

A. Some students have a background, identity, interest, or

talent that is so meaningful they believe their application

would be incomplete without it. If this sounds like you, then

please share your story.

 B. The lessons we take from failure can be fundamental to

later success. Recount an incident or time when you

experienced failure. How did it affect you, and what did you

learn from the experience?

C. Reflect on a time when you challenged a belief or idea. What prompted you to act? Would you make the same decision again?

D. Describe a problem you've solved or a problem you'd like to solve. It can be an intellectual challenge, a research query, or an ethical dilemma - anything that is of personal importance, no matter the scale. Explain its significance to you and what steps you took or could be taken to identify a solution.

E. Discuss an accomplishment or event, formal or informal that marked your transition from childhood to adulthood within your culture, community, or family.

It would be a great idea to use these as practice, and write answers for them in less than 1000, less than 500, and less than 250 words. The reason for the different numbers is different applications use different limitations to see how well

you can get your point across in a certain interval. Also there is

no shame in seeking help or guidance with these. Have your

teacher or parent look over your essay and edit it for any

errors or areas that may confuse the person reading it.

On the following pages are two sample essays written

by Pekin Community High School Students in which you will

be the judge as to the good essay, and the bad essay.

Sample 1:

To Whom It May Concern: I am interested in Illinois

State University. I was glad to read that you like me know that

student motivation and academic preparation are not fully

revealed by a student's high school transcript or by standardized tests.

Highschool bored me, simply it was not challenging, highschool is no longer an institution which can provide an education sufficient to meet the challages of the modern economic situation. A highschool diploma is no longer a document which alone will allow an indivual to attain a job which will support a family. Also, the SAT is no longer a test which divides those who have studied and have made the effort to achieve, from those who bumble through school. At the point books were published on how to pass the SAT, it simply became another test which doesn't prove anything definitely. Because of my viewpoint on highschool and the SAT I did not exert myself on either. I was reserving myself for college. College is the difference which makes the difference.

Of two people applying for the same job, similar in every way except for the fact that one is the holder of a college degree and the other is not, the degree holder is far more likely to get the job. Further, college is where I will learn the knowledge and skills I will use in the workforce of my generation.

I am exciting to be moving into this phase of my life, and look forward to attending your august college.

Sample 2:

Ever since I was little there have always been two careers that have sparked my interest and that I've wanted to pursue. The first career is nursing, which I got from my Aunt who attended Illinois State University. She really enjoyed ISU and loves her nursing job today. We've always been really close and she's inspired me to not only become a nurse, but attend ISU as well. She is the one person in my family whom I have a lot in common with, and it would mean so much to me if I could follow in her footsteps. It would be comforting to know that if I ever had any questions with my classes or even the campus; help from someone I was close to would be just a phone call away. My second career choice is to become a teacher. Many of the teachers I've had in the past have made it quite clear that their job is rewarding and interesting. My one goal in life is to just find something that I would love to do for the rest of my life and stick with it, and that would definitely be accomplished if I went into the education field. I love working with people and could absolutely see myself as being a teacher. Nursing and teaching are two majors that ISU is highly known for, and that is why ISU would fit my needs for a college perfectly. Not only would ISU help me accomplish my educational goals in life, but I already feel at home there. I've

visited ISU many times with my parents and friends, so I know

my way around the campus extremely well. This would make

adjusting to a new home far easier than at any other college. I

feel that the easier I adjust to my new home, the more

successful I would be my freshman year. I already follow

the boys' basketball and football teams for ISU and would love

to go to the games to support them as my own school! I

already wear my ISU spirit wear proudly and cannot wait to

call myself a Red Bird. Fortunately, I already have many

friends who attend ISU, and truthfully, I know I would have a

great experience there. I've recently visited a few different

sororities, and I would be really interested in becoming an

active part of one. Fulfilling my major, being comfortable with

the campus, and being involved are all things that would

contribute to motivating me to work hard. No other college compares to ISU in my mind and it is without a doubt where I would like to be next year.

Which essay do you consider to be the bad essay?

_____

Which essay do you consider to be the good one? Why?

_____

_____

_____

_____

_____

_____

What should/could be changed about the "bad" essay to make it better?

_____

_____

_____

_____

_____

_____

Keep these Tips on writing the best essay question answer handy when doing your own:

- Read the prompt all the way through
- Answer the question the prompt is asking
- Capture the reader's attention early, preferably the first sentence.
- Use complex terms from a thesaurus, but don't go overboard. (Instead of helpful go for advantageous)
- Tell a unique story that will make you memorable.

- Focus on the positives, but mention downfalls as well. Use the downfalls as lessons or turn them into a positive.

- Never go over allotted word count or time if it is timed.

- If possible, compare your story to one of a well-known person in a positive light to help drive the point home, and maybe to shine light on what could be a possible repeat in history.

- Proofread/ revise and edit your work, or have a different set of qualified eyes look it over for you.

- Have an attention grabbing title and first sentence that relates to the story.

- Mention where and how you could possibly fit in at the school, or that particular schools benefit for you.

Do Not Plagiarize!

If it did not come from YOUR own original thoughts cite where you got that information. Be aware YOU can also plagiarize yourself. If YOU write or post something and YOU decide to use that same information in a later work and do not cite the original source it is still plagiarism.

ALL OF THE FOLLOWING ARE CONSIDERED PLAGIARISM:

- Turning in someone else's work as your own
- Copying words or ideas from someone else without giving credit
- Failing to put a quotation in quotation marks
- Giving incorrect information about the source of a quotation
- Changing words but copying the sentence structure of a source without giving credit
- Copying so many words or ideas from a source that it makes up the majority of your work, whether you give credit or not

"Either write something worth reading, or do something worth writing." –Benjamin Franklin-

✓ *Visit a college campus*

Fun Fact: *"Norway has world's highest gas prices. Though they have oil reserves, they don't subsidize fuel and use money to fund free college education and national infrastructure."*

If you have narrowed down your ideal colleges of choice try to visit one of them. If you cannot for any reason, try to visit any local college campus just to see what you are getting yourself into. Most high schools have programs where they do free college visits. Figure out when they are, and sign up for them.

When you get on that college campus make a friend. Rather it is an administrator, or your tour guide, or even just a student passing by.

Make it a point to network with someone who has been where you plan to go!

Get their number, business card, or email. You can use them later to ask questions or even get ahead if it is the right person.

Remember we are transitioning from what you know to whom you know.

You should be jumping with joy by now. You have learned and applied the 10 p's, conquered fear, finessed your SAT, received pockets full of money, and written the dopest application essay ever constructed. Along the way, you realized you have what it takes to be successful, and have gained what you need to sustain you on this journey through the Serengeti of higher learning. There is nothing left to do before you cross that stage but to embody the ideal college student with some tried and true good habits that if practiced consistently can get the desired results.

✓ *Start creating good habits now*

"Excellence is an art won by training and habituation. We do not act rightly because we have virtue or excellence, but we rather have those because we have acted rightly. We are repeatedly what we do. Excellence then, is not an act but a habit. –Aristotle-

What is your best habit:

_____

_____

What is your worse habit:

_____

_____

What do you think could be done to make this habit better:

_____

_____

_____

_____

What most people fail to realize is that your habits define your life. Take for instance a room of 100 people standing up of all different shapes, sizes, and nationalities. You are the center of attention with a microphone in your hands. Directly into that microphone you ask everyone to remain standing who work out at least 5 times a week. Look around. How many people are still standing? Looking at the people who are standing you can see that they have a habit of working out five times a week because they are physically fit, probably have many muscles, or wear really tight shirts. Take a long hard look at your own life and habits, and ask what you can change to be the best, most efficient version of yourself.

Now that YOU have looked at YOURSELF and pinpointed the area YOU need the most help YOU can start now and develop the habits that will get YOU anywhere YOU want to go.

What habits should you aspire to refine you ask?

Have a positive attitude- Attitude controls aptitude. You can only go as high as your attitude will take you. Attitude is a two edged sword that if directed and used correctly can be extremely beneficial in reaching your goals. Take a football player for instance. On the field, he is a steaming locomotive with no fear, and no regard for his opponent. Using attitude in this respect would more than likely make him a great player that leaves an extensive legacy on the field. On the other hand, take that same attitude off the field. Do you think his professors, friends, or fellow students would enjoy being around or helping this person? No, Right? In your life, use your passion to be relentless in the pursuit of your goals, but with people treat them as if they are your most prized possession and watch your life and relationships grow.

Start waking up earlier and having quiet time- There are only 24 hours in every single person's day from the richest to the poorest. If you are wasting or sleeping away most of those hours instead of working toward and meditating on what success is to you how can you expect to succeed? Some places to direct your quiet time are prayer, meditation or yoga, taking a walk with no distractions, or creating and revisiting a vision board. By starting your day on a great note you set the tone for the rest of your day.

Fun Fact: over 90% of millionaires wake up before 8a.m

Eat healthier- your brain is the most powerful muscle in your body, and it is only as good as what you put into it and your body. Meal prepping, though it may be time consuming or boring to your palette it can be a huge help in this area.

Exercise More- If you want to perform at your best you have to assure you are in your top shape. On top of making you, a person of desire exercising improves your brain functions, motor skills, and confidence.

Read More- "poor people have big TVs; successful people have big libraries." Think about it, pretty much anything important you need to know or have desire to find out can be found in a book or an article.

Study Harder- for every hour in class you should spend at least two hours studying and going over what was learned.

Plan Better- Keep a calendar. Keep a planner. Have a daily schedule or to-do list. If you know exactly what you are supposed to be doing at a certain time it will leave less opportunity for you to get off task, stray from your plans, or procrastinate. If you are prepared for what is to come it will be that much easier to conquer.

Procrastination is the kryptonite to success.

Have a vision- Write that vision down with goals and a well thought out plan. Strive to reach those goals. Keep reminders of the future you want, and the (S)Hero's that inspire you toward the future YOU desire. By making your goals and plans visible, it unconsciously makes you work toward them. Make sure you reward yourself when you hit certain milestones.

If you can see it, you can believe it. If you can believe it, you can achieve it!

5 ways to make "IT" stick:

☞ **Commit to doing it thirty days in a row**

☞ **Begin small but continue to grow toward the ultimate goal**

☞ **Write it down and be particular leaving no room for option**

☞ **Create or reimagine some positive triggers/whys**

☞ **Count the cost and realize the consequences**

✓ _**Protect your image and your future with your decisions today.**_

In all these things be careful and make sure you are not putting yourself in a position that can get you in trouble, or drastically alter the outline of your future. Many students make it all the way through high school and lose everything on prom night, or right before they cross the stage. Do not ruin what is supposed to be a storybook ending over something that probably didn't warrant any serious attention in the first place or could have been avoided if _YOU_ had taken a different plan of action.

Social media can be a blessing or a curse!

Everybody tells you don't have a baby, don't do drugs, don't go to jail, or don't skip school. Today, I will tell you DON'T put ANYTHING on SOCIAL MEDIA that could possibly PORTRAY you in a NEGATIVE context.

Here are a few negative connotations that could affect your success and progress later in life.

- *Alcoholic beverages or colored plastic cups*
- *Lewd or nude photos (even in snapchat. Nothing is private, and EVERYTHING can be found again later) #googleyourusername*
- *Inappropriate hand gestures*
- *Risky jokes*
- *Excessive grammatical errors or bad language*
- *Extremely personal or confidential information.*

*Always remember colleges and even potential employers check, and monitor these types of things. You would not want to put yourself in a compromising situation over something so minute. However, if you need to clean your social media image up try **(Social Sweepster)***

Let us round this section off with 9 social media Do's and Don'ts

1) DO post on social media sights regularly, but not to the point that viewers drown you out.

2) DON'T use profanity or other colorful language.

3) DON'T be fake or portray a false depiction of your life.

4) DO practice positivity.

5) DON'T post party or club photos.

6) DON'T post illegal acts and or paraphernalia.

7) DON'T make racist, sexist, or other offensive comments.

8) DON'T complain about or bash others.

9) DO Share positive things you have done or awards you have earned.

Always protect yourself and your future.

What you do today can improve all your tomorrows

–Ralph Marston-

The last thing you must do before moving forward is, "emancipate yourselves from mental slavery, none but ourselves can free our minds." –Marcus Garvey-. The next step on this exciting journey is to "Be FREE" of everything that is holding you back from being the best version of yourself.

"Man is free the moment he wishes to be."

–Voltaire–

Of course, I am here to guide you along this newfound path to freedom. I found that by changing my mind about my attitude, work ethic, and my old way of handling business I started to be happier, more productive, and gained a phonebook filled with people who would drop whatever they were doing to cater to my needs. This caused me to ask myself "Why are people drawn to me, and compelled to help me achieve success in any area I choose?" I found my answer, and created an acronym to go along with this idea of true *freedom.* Let this acronym for being *FREE* be the pillars in which you place upon your already solid foundation to start building your library of success.

✓ *__Be F.R.E.E__*

Be:

F un:

At every stage of your life you should do whatever brings you joy and is fun for you. By doing this, you are creating balance as well as keeping yourself at an elevated state sending out good vibes to the universe. The universe is like a current that is always flowing. Whatever you send out into it rather it is good, bad, or indifferent will always come back to you. It may not return today, this week or even this year, but it will **_ALWAYS_** come back.

Develop a sense of humor. Make people laugh and smile. Be yourself! The right people will gravitate toward you.

There is only and will only ever be one of you. Be the best version of that one-of-a-kind person.

Be:

R eliable:

People are drawn to the people they feel they can trust or count on. If you staple yourself as someone who is reliable, and can get a job done on time and correctly you are sure to be a favorite in many different circles. The most important part to accomplishing this is being a person of your word. Let your Yes mean Yes, and your No mean No. If you say you are going to do something or be somewhere make sure you follow through. Adversely, if you cannot make an appointment or fulfill a promise make sure you communicate that to the necessary people. There is no one thing that will

affect your relationships with people greater than *trust*

Be:

E xcellent:

Being excellent is nothing more than presenting the

best you have to offer. My grandfather a man who worked on

the railroad for 40 years sat me down when I was a young boy

and told me "anything you do that is a representation of you

should be the best representation of you." When you clock

out and walk out the door you should be able to say even 20

years down the road that I made sure everything was correct,

and I put my best foot forward. Take for instance the debacle

with the Samsung Note 7 in 2016. It is a great phone with

many awe-inspiring capabilities, but somewhere down the production line there were some corners cut causing a number of phones to catch on fire putting many innocent people in danger. Do you think the makers of the Note 7 did the best possible job they could, or went back and made sure every intricate detail was done in excellence? What do you think this did to the integrity of the company? Do you assume this company took a major loss in revenue due to this disaster? Do not be a Samsung Note 7 and watch your life catch on fire and burn down everything you have worked for because you were too lazy when it came to being excellent.

Be:

E xcited:

Let everything go! Stop holding on to stuff or letting negative things control your life and your attitude. Yes, I understand that there may be stress, or maybe even you are not in the most favorable environment, and of course, there are always people who get under your skin. However, negativity should have no place in your life.

Be the change you want to see!

Choose to be happy no matter what you face or have faced. Understand everything changes just like the seasons. Winter today could be spring tomorrow. Let your inner light shine bright enough that it is so infectious to others they cannot help but be happy and excited around you. If you struggle here and need someone to talk to, counselors are always there for you. Develop a personal relationship with them, and let them help you through some of those hard times. If need be change your environment. Change the people you hang around, and the things you watch or take part in. Whether you know it or not every person you hang around is taking you somewhere. That destination could be good or bad. It is up to you to decipher if the destination is most favorable for the things you wish to accomplish, and person you hope to be. Ultimately, you make the decisions on if and when to get off the ride. Just like people, the things you watch and listen to regularly affect and mold the person you become. Delete anything from your life that hinders you from smiling. Because...

The most important part of your outfit every day is a smile!

Make sure your smile is always authentic. People will be able to sense if it is not genuine. Give a very heartwarming grateful for life smile. By smiling as if you are already happy you unconscientiously make yourself happy.

Think about it. It could be a lot worse. You could only have one rotting tooth in your mouth. Moreover, if you do only have one tooth left smile anyhow because,

You are beautiful!

"*So please ask yourself: What would I do if I weren't afraid?, and then go do it*"
-Sheryl Sandberg-

"Vision: The act or power of imagination."

-Merriam Webster-

For Johnathan Smith author of *Gulliver's travels* "vision is the art of seeing what is invisible to others." Now, the hard part is drowning out the visions that others have for YOU so YOU can narrow in and focus on YOUR own vision. Having a vision is the most important part of the process of getting to whatever success means for YOU. Here we will start building YOUR vision for YOUR future. If YOU do not have a direction to go YOU could end up anywhere, way off course, or lost. In this next chapter of YOUR life having a vision, and a plan is the most important part of being able to be successful. So together, let us take a trip into YOUR future!

"The only thing worse than being blind is having sight and no vision" -Hellen Keller-

<u>Vision Building Exercise:</u>

In five years where do I see myself

_____

_____

_____

_____

_____

_____

In ten years where do I see myself

_____

_____

_____

_____

_____

If I could live one place in the world for the rest of my life where would I live

_____

_____

If money did not matter, and I could have one job for the rest of my life and be happy, but not get paid for it what would it be?

_____

_____

What are my top 3 job choices in order of interest?

1. _____

2. _____

3. _____

Life hack 101: The Ultimate Guide to College Success

What is the dream salary I want to make per year

_____

Name my top five colleges in order of most favorite

1. _____

2. _____

3. _____

4. _____

5. _____

If I had a million dollars what would be the first 3 things I

would do with my money

_____

_____

_____

_____

_____

What awards or accolades would I like to gain in my life?

_____

_____

_____

_____

What five words are most important to me that I think

everyone should live his or her life by

_____

_____

If I could have my life summed up in one sentence on my

tombstone, what would that sentence be

_____

_____

_____

Now, YOU have a rough draft or a foundation for YOUR life vision that YOU can begin to build on. Write it down, make it visual, and verbally remind YOURSELF every day. Print out pictures, and put reminders of YOUR vision all around YOU. Along YOUR journey whatever that may be, keep in mind the words of business guru Joel A. Barker.

"Vision without action is merely a dream. Action without vision just passes the time. Vision with action can CHANGE THE WORLD!"

Part 2:

Game

Time

"Every year, many, many stupid people graduate college.

And if they can do it, so can you."

-John Green-

College is one of the hardest uphill climbs you will

ever have to face in your life. It is a period that challenges

you, grows you, prepares you, and truly stresses you out. Here

you may fall in love. You may lose friends. You may gain

weight. You may try some things you never thought you

would do in your lifetime. You may curse. You may pull your

hair out. You may have to learn how to survive off 20 dollars for a whole month. You could possibly be placed in a pressure cooker that breaks you down lower than you ever wanted to go. If this is the case keep in mind that without pressure diamonds are nothing more than a lump of coal.

At the beginning of my college journey, I was lost, but eventually it started coming together. My self-esteem had taken some major shots along the way. My college experience was fueled with highs and lows. I fell in love. I made friends. We broke up... I searched for validation. I made A's, but I also failed some classes I stayed up all night and studied extremely hard for.

People believed that I felt or thought I was better than they were not because I was mean spirited or stuck-up, but because I was always smiling, making people laugh, confident, and people were drawn to me. I had nice things, but I worked hard for those commodities. I still felt alone, and I was overly self-conscious.

I made money, but I worked 40+ hours every week on top of my schoolwork load of at times 18 credit hours. I had missed numerous birthdays, holidays, and special occasions. I traveled across the U.S met many people and made many friends, but even with all of this I still didn't feel important or validated and turned to alcohol, drugs, and women to cope. In those years of my life, I was struggling to find myself, drowning in my bad decisions, afraid to seek help because I felt embarrassed and thought no one would understand.

When you feel no one can relate keep in mind nothing is new under the sun, and countless students have been at this exact point before you. I can honestly say first-hand how I coped with these feelings *is not the way.* You can run, hide in your room, or maybe try to numb yourself to your problems.

Eventually you will have to deal with your issues or they will deal with you.

Personally, to get myself out of this hole I had dug in my life I chose to believe in a benevolent Universe, which has a grand master plan for me (and for everything else). I have found this belief to suit me best; it helps me see anything that's happening as a part of this plan. This new awareness helped me to realize there is a light on the inside of me, and I stopped trying to dim it to make others feel comfortable around me. I went through this hardship first hand, and wasted *A LOT* of time and money.

You don't have to waste time, effort, money, or emotions!

You should never have to dim your light.

No matter what you believe. Rather it is in the flow of the universe, Karma, Buddha, or like for me God through Jesus Christ. They all have a different way of teaching the same thing. Which is there is a light in all of us that shines. It grows brighter when we are happy, when we excel, when we know who we are, when we are confident in ourselves but still humble enough not to think we are better than others, and most of all when we are kind and helpful to our peers and even strangers. No matter whom you believe the messenger to be, take this message and _Let your light shine_. It does you absolutely no good to harp on failures. LIVE your best life NOW and for the rest of your days. Start here! Start today!

Do you wish you had a trick to finish everything you start to the best of your ability?

✓ **Do not. I repeat DO NOT procrastinate**

Procrastination without a doubt kills the possible success of a college student. Wayne Gretzky one of the greatest hockey players to slide onto the ice put it like this "Procrastination is one of the most common and deadliest of diseases and its toll on happiness and success is heavy."

I know I KNOW you may say... "But I work better under pressure, Why rush I have time, they are not grading this anyway, I'll get it done." All of these things are excuses and most times lies we tell ourselves to help cope with our sickness, but what I would say to that is...

"Excuses are tools of the incompetent used to build monuments of nothingness. Those who specialize in them are seldom good at anything." -Unknown-

Every college student has lied to themselves at least once before graduating by saying, "I will finish it in the morning." #NewsFlash, No you will not. Or if you do it will be a rush job, and not your best effort. One of America's founding fathers, Benjamin Franklin had this disease the worst until one day he made up his mind and told himself, "Don't put off until tomorrow what you can do today." That day his life changed and we will forever remember all of his great accomplishments. Adopt his mindset, practice it until it becomes habit, and watch as the successes come!

There will be endless opportunities for you to indulge in something a lot more intriguing than course work. LIKE SLEEP, or social media, YouTube, or binge watching TV series on Netflix and Hulu. Whatever you do, do not take the bait. Give your best effort to ***Get ahead and stay ahead!*** Use these tips to help you keep your eye on the prize.

How To Kick procrastination's butt:

- o Pick ONE THING to focus on at a time

- o Start today being optimistic with where you are

- o Start small. Pick something you can do towards the ultimate goal and do it for a short spurt regularly

- o Remove all distractions, seclude yourself, then set a timer for one hour while you work. After the timer goes off reward yourself a ten to twenty-minute break. Do as many sets of this as you can

o   Listen to motivational videos or music while you work

o   Don't overload yourself or schedule *(Quality over Quantity)*

o   Have an accountability partner

o   Be disciplined

o   HAVE FUN!

o   Most important of all PRIORITIZE!

Right now stop what you're doing, get a piece of paper and a pen. On that piece of paper, make a list of 5 to 7 things that are important to you including school. I will also make a sample list to help with this illustration. My list would look something like,

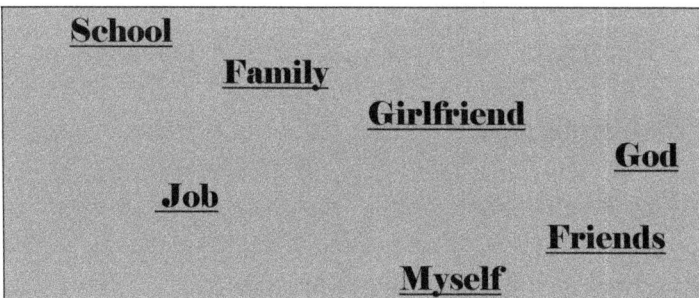

School

Family

Girlfriend

God

Job

Friends

Myself

Now, take that same list and put it in order from most important to least important. I know this may be hard, and it may hurt some people that are close to you, but if they truly love you they will understand. My list would look something like...

1. God	5. My Job
2. Myself	6. Girlfriend
3. Family	7. Friends
4. School	

Once you prioritize your life that should remain the order to your life; govern your decisions and manage your time as need be based on these priorities. Use this technique to help schedule your priorities or To-do list. Of course, there may be times when adjustments and exceptions can be made like holidays, special occasions, or even homecoming. However, by being consistent in following this flow you are practicing discipline, and creating the most important habit you will need to learn for this time in your life.

Discipline = Doing what you HAVE to do now so you can do what you WANT to do later!

Conquering the discipline obstacle is imperative to success at any level in college and your life. Discipline is how you will win that bothersome battle with procrastination. A man who had a very good relationship with words said this on the subject, *"Procrastination makes easy things hard and hard things harder." – Mason Cooley-* This is exactly why procrastination has killed the careers of countless people especially students.

Start now, and cultivate a plan and schedule for your life. Then discipline your mind to carry out this task consistently each day. Don't worry if you miss a day or mess up. Don't beat yourself up. Just dust yourself off get up and keep pushing forward until you cross every goal of yours off that list.

✓ *Handle Financial Aid As Soon As Possible*

This should be one of the first things you take care of before stepping on your college campus, as well as while you are on campus. You need to have a plan on how to pay for school. You cannot get a grade in a class that you cannot pay for. Follow this plan of action and you will be set up with time to spare before your first class even starts and hopefully with more money than you know what to do with it.

1. ***Fill out your Fafsa early and get it to your school's office of financial aid.*** Many times, it is first come first serve. Remember the early bird gets the worm every time.

2. ***Follow up with a financial aid advisor***

A. Every school has different financial aid advisors that help you through this process. Pick one you can get along with and make them your point of contact. Only communicate through the same person unless you absolutely have to go to someone else.

B. Going to the same person creates a special connection and relationship that could help expedite your process later, or even get you more resources.

Don't Forget: "It's not always what you know, but who you know."

3. Finalize financial aid A.S.A.P

A. Lines get longer and money gets shorter the more you procrastinate with this process. You don't have to wait until your family files their taxes. Start early, take advantage of the new OCT. 1st early application registration for the FAFSA

4. Scholarship applications

B. Every school has general scholarships available to everyone. These are competitive so maintain a high GPA, be at the front of the line, and get to know the school's scholarship administrator. (Even if you just stop by once a week to follow up, re-introduce yourself, or just say "Hi") The more these people see you the more you will be on their mind when they are actually making monetary decisions.

C. Your particular field of study may offer scholarships. You can get these the same way by applying and being persistent. Also getting involved with your declared major specific organizations could benefit you.

D. Go outside your comfort zone and stay up to date on events. Some schools hold pageants, competitions, or even days where they award scholarships just for being in a certain place at a certain time. Find out if your school offers any of these and try it out. You never know it could change your life.

"You will enrich your life immeasurably if you approach it with a sense of wonder and discovery, and always challenge yourself to try new things." –Nate Berkus-

✓ *Choose the right Path for YOU*

"There is not ONE path. There is not even the RIGHT path. There is only YOUR path--- and you know it's yours by how it feels to you" -Sue Krebs-

Probably the most frightening part of college for most people is declaring a major. This may be for many different reasons like fear to choose the wrong one, fear of how hard it may be, outside influences like mentors and parents, or just because this pretty much could decide the rest of your life. Scary right? Nevertheless, it doesn't have to be.

Take for instance Bill Gates, J.K. Rowling, and LeBron James. What do they have in common? The first thing that will come to mind is that they have a lot of money. Why do they have all of this money? The simple answer is that they are really good at what they do. If you go deeper, it's because they love what they do. Grasp this, just like the three people listed above you can make any amount of money if you do what you love and humble yourself to the process of becoming great at it. In honor of these three people the only three commandments you need to follow when choosing a major are...

1. <u>Pick something you love</u> *(LeBron James)*
2. <u>Pick something you could do the rest of your life for free and be happy if money didn't matter</u> *(J.K. Rowling)*
3. <u>Choose something you are really good at or interested in</u> *(Bill Gates)*

Anything YOU do if you master it and become an expert at it YOU can live comfortably or make as much money as YOU choose. So try not to let those quick moneymakers or safe jobs like engineering, accounting, or nursing cross your mind if you are not passionate about it because you will be miserable. This feeling will set you up to possibly not even finish college. When it comes to choosing a major an end goal and vision are important. If you cannot see YOUR future in the path you have chosen you won't have the passion to get to the finish line.

Now that we have the criteria, let's narrow down our choices: In the chart on the next page the three commandments are given with space for you to fill in the top things that meet each set of criteria for YOU!

Something you love doing	Something that makes you happy doing it	Something you are talented at doing

Use this table to guide you on your career path decision. Don't worry about how much "people" say you will make, or the people who can't see your dreams coming true because this journey is only yours to take. (Side note: If you have a single thing that fits all three criteria that is indeed your purpose in life.) Don't get in the way of what your heart is pushing you towards.

"Follow your heart. Your heart is your GPS for life's journey. It will never lead you anywhere you are not meant to be."

-Jordan Ball-

Now that you have an idea of where you want to go it is time to take action and develop a plan on how to get there. Pablo Picasso an above average artist of his day told himself daily that "Action is the foundational key to success." A wise person learns from those before him. Follow the blueprint other successful individuals have left while traveling their own personal journey.

✓ _Set yourself up for success on YOUR chosen path_

The first thing you need to do to set you up for success on this road you will travel is to know your degree plan.

Your degree plan is your road map.

Without knowing the ins and outs of getting through your major to that coveted degree you will end up lost, in a place you have no business being, or in the quitter's circle.

Any degree plan is easy to find just go to your schools **course catalogue**. There everything will be laid out from length of degree, suggested classes to take and when, number of hours to take each semester to stay on the plan, if a minor is required, who to talk to as far as department heads, and where you need to go.

Next, find your advisor, get to know them, and ask questions. Your advisor is your Co-pilot on this smooth sailing flight through undergrad. Make sure you know exactly what they are doing, and that their actions line up with your plan.

Questions to ask your advisor

1. *What and Why?*

- Always ask what they are doing and why they are doing what they are doing. The more familiar you become with this process the better you can do it on your own so that when registration comes back around you won't have to make appointments or wait in lines. Also two sets of eyes are always better than one when searching for an error.

2. *Do I have to worry about my degree requirements changing?*

- Sometimes department heads meet and decide to add or take away from a major's degree plan. Know if this happens often, and if it does will it affect the people who have already started or just the incoming students.

3. *Is a minor required with my major?*

- If it is, here you can experiment or set yourself up for a feasible plan B. Say you are a communications major and may want to teach later. Pick a minor that you may be interested in teaching and it will pay off for you in the long run. Keep in mind that different minors have different requirements.

4. *What professors do students usually prefer for different classes?*

- This could help you eliminate taking a class where you can barely understand or keep up with what is going on. Or even a professor who is just plain rude. If your professor is passionate about what they do it will ignite that same passion in you.

5. *Are there any alternate classes I can take to fulfill the requirements for my degree?*

- There could be an easier or more interesting class that could substitute another and still count toward the completion of your degree.

- College is a time that can be extremely busy, stressful, and demanding especially with you being on your own. You don't need to add any more to your plate by taking unnecessarily challenging courses you are not passionate about. Use this time to broaden your horizon and explore just a little bit.

6. *What class if any is semi- occasional?*

- Most times the further you get down your degree plan the course class size you need may be smaller making it harder to get a seat in that section, or a course may only come around occasionally. So plan accordingly.

✓ **7 Habits of Highly Effective College Students**

"Be the one to stand out in the crowd" –Joel Osteen-

Still today, the most asked question on any college campus happens to be "Are there any extra credit opportunities?" Even if the professor for that class says no, there is still an opportunity to put you over the top in any course you find yourself taking. How is this possible you ask? I guess you will just have to wait and see.

Stephen R. Covey is a world-renowned author who is well known for his best seller *"7 Habits of Highly Effective People."* The book opens by explaining how many individuals who have achieved a high degree of success find themselves still struggling with an inner need for developing personal effectiveness and growing healthy relationships with other people.

Covey believes the way we see the world is entirely based on our own perceptions. In order to change a given situation, we must change ourselves, and in order to change ourselves, we must be able to change our perceptions. I used this idea and developed from my experiences and the experiences of many others what it takes to be a success in your studies, relationally sound, and an overall effective college student. Outlined are the seven habits for being an effective student.

ONE. ***Make others feel important.***

A. Get to know the people in your courses and your professor. Make yourself visible and available enough so these people know exactly who you are.

B. Stop by your professor's office for tutoring, to ask
    questions, and just to say Hi. This comes in handy
    especially during a curve if any. In addition, read their
    research and inquire about it. Try and connect it to the
    class material.

C. Support your classmate's endeavors that go beyond
    the classroom. Making others feel important makes
    them want to cater to you.

TWO.   <u>Put learning first and be engaged.</u>

A. This means sit as close as possible to the front, and
    stay awake.

B. Give off positive body language, and pleasant facial
    expressions.

C. Nod in agreement some times when your professor looks at you even if you are lost, but be conscious you're not a bobble head mindlessly nodding.

D. Take detailed notes, and record the lecture

E. Ask relevant questions

F. Have intelligent interjections, and opinions in class lectures or discussions

G. Even if you party all night, make sure above all things you make it to class. My biggest rule in college was we party hard, but we study harder. No matter what get to class. Even if you have to wear the same clothes, put on some dark shades, or sleep outside the classroom. Make the effort to make it there.

H. **Stay off your phone.**

I. Remove any distraction and or person outside of the classroom from your life that takes away from your learning experience.

THREE. *Dress with your future in mind.*

A. NO Pajamas!!! Some things are only meant to be worn at home. Wearing these things to class sends the message that you are not interested, and not making the necessary preparations to ensure your success. Repeat this in the mirror to yourself every morning before you start your day. *"You look good, you feel good, you feel good you perform good."*

B. Try to keep personal views and opinions outside of the classroom. They could have a negative affect if your professors oppose with those views.

C. It is ok to have pride for your culture, but keep it positive. Opt to wear a Martin Luther King shirt as opposed to Malcolm X holding a gun. Refrain from clothing with vulgarity, or profanity. I respect your love for seeing art in any form, but others may not be as apt to accept your views. Every representation of you is sending a message whether you intend to or not.

Aim to make all the signals, vibes, and representations of yourself that you present to others the best most genuine representation. Even if you have to play the game and conform just a little bit to get ahead. Different is good. Too different makes others uncomfortable.

D.   Business owners, managers, and professors have expressed that the more formal their clothing is the more respect their opinions get. Inside the classroom, business casual is a great happy medium.

FOUR.   **_Be Proactive stay two or three chapters ahead of the class Work on assignments immediately._**

In the age of technology we find ourselves in, almost all professors keep lecture materials online. Find those materials before your semester even starts and get ahead. By doing this, you are becoming familiar with the course information, and putting yourself in a position to better engage and impress your professor inside the classroom. Also if things come up leaving you less study time later in the semester you are

already prepared.

FIVE. <u>**Sharpen your brain and read**</u>

This is only for illustration purposes to get you the reader

to visualize the tone of this quote. Before you read it, imagine

a 5'2" Middle Eastern man from India with a heavy accent

who has a dry sense of humor, but every now and then tries to

be funny. I say this because I think that is why this quote from

one of my engineering professors during one of my hardest

semesters stuck with me.

"Uh reading is uh brain feeding." –Dr. Shakir-

This was absolutely true then and especially now.

Wealth and knowledge is found in books, and articles written after much research. These are the types of information outlets you should partake in on a regular basis instead of the fallacies in social media reporting.

Most millionaires and billionaires read at least one to two books a month. So should you.

Some of your professors may have even written a book, or done some research that led to them publishing a couple dissertations. Try your best to find things like that and ask them questions about their research during class if it relates, or even spark a conversation in free time after class. This is that cherry on top that will give you a lot of favor with each professor. Be genuine, and not annoying. Have maybe one or two questions, and let them lead the conversation!

SIX. STUDY STUDY STUDY

A. Put at least two hours of studying in for each one hour of lecture time. Add an hour for the classes that are more challenging to you.

B. Do not try to cram this is not high school. Set time aside to study a little at a time instead of trying to force yourself to learn everything the night before.

C. Have a balanced study group. There should be someone smarter than you that you can ask questions, as well as someone not as smart that you can help teach. Because the more you teach it and repeat it the better you learn it.

TIP: Chewing the same flavor gum when taking a test as you did while studying, and writing in blue ink helps you remember things better!

SEVEN. <u>*Show up and show out!*</u>

A. Be there on time and be aware of what's going on. This shows you respect a person's time, and you are grateful for the opportunities you have been afforded.

If you're on time, you're late. If you're early, you're on time.

B. Do your best. If your present best is not good enough make the necessary adjustments to empower you to do better. If this means skipping outings and parties to study, do it. If you have to find a tutor, do it. If you have to stay after class to ask for clarity from the professor, DO IT!

C. Sometimes to get ahead it is even possible to sit in on classes before you actually take them. Make sure you clear it with the professor first so you do not offend them in any way.

D. Be confident you will succeed

You can and you will do anything you set your mind and actions toward. It may not come fast, or even in the same timing as others around you, but when the time is right it will come no matter how far or how big that goal may seem. Don't get weary, *just keep swimming, just keep swimming, just keep swimming, swimming, swimming*!

We have reached the end. Our quest has been inspiring, informative, fun, and above all else memorable. It has been my pleasure helping you get it right where I got it all wrong. We have learned, who to be, how to be, what to do, where to go, who to talk to, and what to say. You now have everything

you will need and more to build a sturdy foundation for

your library of success in college and life. Once you have

accomplished cultivating all of this newfound knowledge,

and practice what you have learned on a consistent basis,

the final step is to bring it all together with a set of rules to

govern yourself by.

⭐ *The Golden Rules for College* ⭐

1. **Be Persistent:** not everything will happen right away or

    on the first try. Remember F.A.I.L means First Attempt

    In Learning. If at first you don't succeed, try until you

    get it.

2. **Develop core values that keep you grounded:** Some examples include; be excellent, stay humble, treat others as you want to be treated, and be proactive. When you are making your own list, it should include the basis of characteristics you want to embody, and govern every encounter you have or decision you make.

3. **Get Involved:** There are endless amounts of opportunities on campus that can help others, or help you network and gain skills you don't already have. Try some of them!

4. **Have school spirit:** You spend a lot of time and money here. Why not love it. If you love it, you will perform

better. It's a fact alumnae who could be very influential pay attention to people they feel love their alma mater just as much as they do.

5. **Always be aware of your surroundings:** Explore and be familiar with your campus. You never know what interesting things you could see or find. You may even find shortcuts to places you have been taking the scenic route to reach. On the other hand, and most importantly make sure you know where you are, who is around you, and a few exit plans just in case something out of your control occurs. Take the necessary safety measures to ensure you make it back home.

"Life is not measured in the breaths we take, but by the

moments that take our breath away."

–Unknown-

6. **Make friends:** Have a core group of like-minded

    people with similar values. Do your best to aim for

    diversity when choosing people to connect with. If you

    are only with people who are exactly like you then you

    put yourself in a position where you cannot grow

    outside of your comfort zone.

7.

With this remember life and karma is funny. You never know

whom you may need or when you may need a person so do

not burn any bridges.

These friends are important because they help create memories that will be reminisced on until it is time to leave this earth, and they become your accountability partners who keep you in line with your goals.

8. **Have Balance:** Set some time to relax, and even party. Don't go overboard to the point your free time affects your work ethic, or scholastic endeavors.

9. ***If you have one drink, it is no longer consensual:*** Protect yourself, protect your school, protect the people around you, and most importantly protect your legacy.

10. <u>**Social media can be your best friend or your worst enemy, use it wisely:**</u> Always Always Always keep in mind that perception is everything as it relates to your future success. Social media **CAN be** used as a positive conduit for you. You could gain recognition, friends, learn new stuff, and even see things you may have otherwise never had a chance to see. Adversely, there is a dark side of social media that is seldom addressed. ***EVERYTHING you post on any social medium can be seen or found at any time FOREVER!*** Imagine trying to get a job right out of college and your future boss does a social media search on you, *which they always do*. Would they think what was found would be a positive reflection of what their company stands for? Would they like what they see? Could what they see be shown

in a board room meeting and have a positive influence? If you say no, start today and make changes that will empower your future. If you need extra help go to social sweepster. Also phones have become a big distractor. Often times we find ourselves so consumed by them and what they offer we miss out on life and the experiences around us. Control your phone don't let it control you. Don't be the person who scrolls through timelines and looks up only to find 3 hours has passed and they are no closer to their goals.

11. ***Don't send nudes:*** Don't do anything that can come back and bring shame to you, the people close to you, or your university.

I have watched people lose jobs, opportunities, get expelled from school, and their whole life change based on one dumb decision.

12. **Learn to cook/ make do with what you have/ and save money:** Eating out on a regularly adds up over time. You can save thousands of dollars a year by just cooking.

13. **Develop a clear line between *WANTS* and *NEEDS:*** This is another area where discipline has to be in the driver's seat. You have to have a switch that clicks on and says do I really need this or am I unnecessarily splurging for one reason or another.

14. **Books are not always mandatory:** but if they are there are better ways than selling your soul.

A. Get an older version of the same book. Most times only a few lines and pictures are changed in the new copies.

B. Renting the book could be a cheaper option for a semester than purchasing that book

C. Order online- www.Amazon.com, www.valorebooks.com, www.chegg.com, www.hpb.com

D. Bill Gates created a free textbook website that is https://openstax.org your books could possibly be there

E. Book vouchers could be given out or book scholarships at your school

F. Make friends with a book store employee and use their discount

G. Ask your professor if they might have an extra copy of the book that you can borrow for the semester

15. **Try not to work a real job unless you have to:** Studies have shown that students who work longer hours perform less well academically. Grades usually drop one letter grade per 15 hours a week worked. School is already a full time job, do your best not to add to that load. If you do have to work, try to opt for Work-study. This helps toward housing or tuition and your employers on campus are more lenient because they understand your main responsibility in school.

16. **In college sleep is a luxury that can be performed anywhere except class at any time and every one will understand**

17. <u>Exercise regularly:</u> You pay for it so you might as well get your money's worth! Exercising regularly benefits your body, mind, and confidence.

18. **<u>Get to know your college president and vice president:</u>** These are very prestigious people who may be able to help you in the future. Drop by every now and then and say Hi. Or even pass on some ideas of how the campus could run smoother. With them and everybody else you meet a way to leave a lasting good impression is learn their name and call them by it, compliment them on something they are wearing, have achieved, or ask about something you know that they are adamant about and listen to understand not

to be understood. If you do these things, you will be sure to get on that individuals good side.

19. **<u>Learn Time Management:</u>** Time is of the essence. Time is one of the few things you cannot get back once it is spent. Think of time as money. If you only had 24 dollars a day that had to be spent each day, and did not roll over how would you spend it. Would you waste it on frivolous items that do not retain value and that you don't necessarily need? On the other hand, would you buy the things you need and spend that money wisely? Each day you are given a new 24 dollars except it is in the form of hours. You cannot get it back, and all of it is spent by the end of the day. Prioritize

your time well enough that you have something to show for it when all of your hours spent are added up.

20. **Respect your roommate:** Here that Golden Rule that says, "Treat others the way you want to be treated," applies more than ever. In college, it is inevitable that you will have a roommate at some point. Nobody wants that annoying, dirty, inconsiderate roommate who uses all of their things without asking. Keep this in mind and be the best roomie you could possibly be. Sit down and talk the first week to set a few ground rules because everyone is different in what they preference. A few guidelines to help the roommate situation go over well could be...

☆ If you use the last of it replace it, especially toilet paper. Nobody wants to get to the end of that Chipotle from last night and look over to see there is no TP on the roll.

☆ If you cook, clean. It would probably be best to have days where each roommate cleans communal areas. Cleaning schedule is key.

"Cleanliness is next to Godliness"

☆ Ask before you use my things. EVERYTIME! I don't care if I said you could have a bowl of my Cap'n Crunch yesterday. I may not be feeling as giving today.

☆ If the trash is full and you see it ___Take It Out.___

☆ Give fair warning before having more than one guest, sleepovers, or parties.

☆ Be mindful of the noise level especially during bedtime.

☆ If my door is closed, I'm not open for conversation. If it is cracked, it's a green light.

☆ Does everyone chip in on communal items including groceries, or is one person in charge of certain items.

☆ Give at least a month notice if one is moving out.

21. **Pray and meditate:** Whether you believe there is a higher power or not you should have some alone time where you reflect and regroup. It's like driving a car. If you drive and drive eventually you will run out of gas and have to fill up. Practice this often to ensure that you don't burn out at a critical moment in your life.

22. **<u>Pay It Forward:</u>** Your life, your experiences, and your failures are not just your own, but are to be used to help someone else. Do anything in your power to build the bridge and help someone behind you get over that troubled water you had to wade through.

23. **<u>Leave A Legacy:</u>** The campus, the people who come in contact with you, and the people who come after you should be changed in some way for the better by you being there. Use your talents, skills, and ideas. Let your light shine and make a difference somehow someway. Don't follow the same paths that have been there, blaze a new trail!!!

Legacy is greater than currency

"Though no one can go back and make a brand new start, anyone

can start from now and make a brand new ending."

-Carl Bard-

"Focus on the journey, not the destination. Joy is found not in

finishing an activity but in doing it."

--Greg Anderson-

Helpful Resources

"Success is not about resources. It's about how resourceful you are with what you have."

–Tony Robbins-

Volunteering

www.volunteermatch.com

www.createthegood.org

www.bgca.org **(Boys and Girls Club of America)**

College applications

www.Commonapp.org

www.Universalcollegeapp.com

www.ApplyTexas.org

commonblackcollegeapp.com

bigfuture.collegeboard.org/get-in/applying-101/applying-to-college-faq

Financial Aid

https://studentaid.ed.gov/sa/types **(Different types of financial aid)** https://fafsa.ed.gov/ **(Free Application for Federal Student Aid)**

www.Zinch.com

www.scholarships.com

www.fastweb.com

www.nextstudent.com

(Scholly) Scholarship app for smart phones

Textbooks

www.Amazon.com

www.valorebooks.com

www.chegg.com

www.hpb.com

Bill gates created a free textbook website that is
https://openstax.org

Other

www.ratemyprofessors.com **(This sites lets students grade their professors publically)**

http://www.lifehack.org/articles/technology/21-most-useful-websites-every-college-student-needs-know.html **(21 websites you may need for college)**

Things you could do with your major can be found here

https://bigfuture.collegeboard.org/majors-careers

Below is a website where a number of FREE SAT materials can be found.

www.powerscore.com/sat/help/content_practice_tests.cfm

"Reading is to the mind what exercise is to the body."

-Joseph Addison-

You Are What You Read

- ❖ "The Secret"
  By Rhonda Byrne
- ❖ "Oh The Places You'll Go"
  By Dr. Seuss
- ❖ "7 Habits of Highly Effective People"
  By Stephen R. Covey
- ❖ "The Alchemist"
  By Paulo Coelho
- ❖ "The Secret to Success"
  By Eric Thomas
- ❖ "The Millionaire's Secrets: Life Lessons in Wisdom and Wealth"
  By Mark Fisher
- ❖ "The Art of Implementation: How to do Things That You've Always Wanted to do"
  By Michael S. Pittman

"He that loves reading has everything within his reach"

-William Godwin-

Self Portrait

Name:_____

Date of Birth: _____

Motto:

_____

_____

_____

High School Attended/College Attending:

_____

Graduation Date _____ # of Brothers _____

# of Sisters _____

Mothers Best Advice:

_____

_____

_____

Fathers Best Advice:

_____

_____

_____

Talents:

_____

_____

Dream Job:

_____

Dream Car:

_____

Favorite College:

_____

Best Habit:

_____

Hobbies/Interest:

_____

_____

Most Valued Possession:

_____

The Person Who had the most impact on my life:

_____

If I gave the Commencement Speech at Graduation, my

Topic/Theme would be

_____

Your **(S)**hero: (The person you could see yourself being in 5-10 years)

_____

My Favorites:

Movie: _____

Comedian: _____

Actor: _____

 Actress: _____

Television Show:_____

Sport: _____

Athlete: _____

Food: _____

Color: _____

Book: _____

Author: _____

Song: _____

Singer/Group (Male): _____

(Female): _____

Place you go to think:_____

The last book I read (for Pleasure): _____

I really regret:

_____

_____

_____

_____

The 4 Guest from present or past that would be at my fantasy

dinner are?

_____

_____

_____

_____

If I were reincarnated, I would be...

_____

_____

You have the power to be what you've always wanted and dreamt of being. You just don't know yet how to harness it. You've gotten lost in what other people said and expected. You've been lied to about your potential and you've been held down because other people are afraid of the great person you could become. Why? Because success holds a mirror up to their failures. That's why people want you to follow the same path that they do. They either didn't dream big enough, or they were too scared to go after their dreams. Now they want you to think that you can't accomplish your goals either. Well, guess what? You AREN'T them. You are your own person, and you have the ability to create the life that you've always wanted. It's always been in you. It's time to let it out. **—Les Brown "Laws of Success"-**

Recommended Affirmations:

See It Through

By Edgar Albert Guest

When you're up against a trouble,

Meet it squarely, face to face;

Lift your chin and set your shoulders,

Plant your feet and take a brace.

When it's vain to try to dodge it,

Do the best that you can do;

You may fail, but you may conquer,

See it through!

Black may be the clouds about you

And your future may seem grim,

But don't let your nerve desert you;

Keep yourself in fighting trim.

If the worst is bound to happen,

Spite of all that you can do,

Running from it will not save you,

See it through!

Even hope may seem but futile,

When with troubles you're beset,

But remember you are facing

Just what other men have met.

You may fail, but fall still fighting;

Don't give up, whate'er you do;

Eyes front, head high to the finish

See it through!

<u>Invictus</u>

By William Ernest Henley

Out of the night that covers me,

Black as the pit from pole to pole,

I thank whatever gods may be

For my unconquerable soul.

In the fell clutch of circumstance

I have not winced nor cried aloud.

Under the bludgeoning's of chance

My head is bloody, but unbowed.

Beyond this place of wrath and tears

Looms but the Horror of the shade,

And yet the menace of the years

Finds and shall find me unafraid.

It matters not how strait the gate,

How charged with punishments the scroll,

I am the master of my fate,

I am the captain of my soul.

<u>Stand Up!</u>

Treat others like you want to be treated. Don't be an innocent bystander as others are ridiculed, stepped on, or taken advantage of. Stand up for what you believe! Stand up for those who are too weak or cannot stand up for themselves! Do Not be silenced. Use your voice and actions to change the world You are a super hero. Someone out there needs your saving. Don't let fear of losing, getting hurt, or dealing with what your peers may say and think stop you from doing what you believe is right. Don't back down. Set your feet in the face of opposition and fight as if YOUR life depended on it. You may not win the battle, but with persistence you shall claim overall victory in the war!

"EMPTY YOUR BUCKET"

GIVE YOUR ALL! Make sure at the end of it all that there is nothing left for you to give. Make it a priority to give everything and everybody the very best that you have to offer each and every time.

Where is the wealthiest place on Earth?

It's the graveyard. There, many ideas never came to be, many creative inventions were never constructed for one reason or another. Make sure that you are not the person that dies with your bucket full or even half-full of potential. *GO FULL SPEED. GIVE 110%, PUSH UNTIL SOMETHING MOVES.*

Don't let fear, or failure, or the opinions of others including family hold you back. *YOU CAN DO IT.* No matter what *IT* is. Confucius once prophesied "He who says he can and he who says he can't are both usually right." Don't be the person saying or thinking you can't. You can do, achieve, or go anywhere as long as you believe you can and are willing to put forth the effort. When you put your mind to it and direct your life towards it *NOTHING CAN STOP YOU!*

HAVE NO REGRETS

LIVE EACH DAY AS IF IT'S YOUR LAST

ABOVE ALL ENJOY THE JOURNEY

<u>Finish the Race</u>

<u>DON'T QUIT!!!</u> If you still have breath in your lungs, blood pumping into your veins, a functioning brain, and movement in your limbs **you can continue the fight**. The pain or discomfort you feel is temporary, but if you give up now it will last forever. Just because you can't see the finish line does not mean it is not there. It only means you are still becoming a champion. Do not give in to fear, or listen to your exhausted emotions that will lead you to believe you can't go any further. You would rather die than get to the future wishing you didn't give up today realizing the finish line was only a few more steps, only one more hurdle away. Give it your all, and let nothing but death come between you and your goals. Remember success may not always mean winning or being the best, but success **IS ALWAYS** found when you **<u>cross the finish line!</u>**

Repeat this to yourself every day!

I CAN!

I WILL!

I MUST!

FIGHT TO THE FINISH!

NO MATTER HOW BAD IT IS OR
HOW BAD IT GETS. I'M GOING
TO MAKE IT!

"Ask and it will be given to you, seek and you shall find, knock and the door will be opened unto you."

-Matthew 7:7-

"Keep your face always toward the sunshine- and shadows will fall behind you."

-Walt Whitman-

Reflection

<u>*Ideas for reflection could include:*</u>

What did I learn? What sparked me and related to me or made me think? What did I learn that could help someone else? What do I need to do better to ensure my success? Your experiences applying the knowledge gained from this book.

Reflection

<u>Note to Self</u>

Have you ever thought, "what if I could go back to my past and relive it with all the knowledge that I have now?" If you are anything like me, you have thought about it more than once. This section of the book is dedicated to those same visionaries. A handful of people from different backgrounds and universities dug deep to foster a special message they would leave for themselves, and future college students to help guide them along their college journey!

Texas State 2014

8th grade science Teacher

Have fun/enjoy life, Networking is key, Change your major

Dear Vicky,

What's up girl! I know you are working, but please do not forget to enjoy your time in college. It's okay to step out of the box and socialize with others. College is all about balance, not just academics as you know it. Also, look for more scholarships. Student loans are NOT what you want. Trust me. They are evil.

Sincerely,

Vicky Roshell

Raven S. Moody

Indiana University
August 2016: Bachelors of Arts in Journalism,
Author & multi-media journalist

• Get involved in extra circulars and take advantage of any opportunity to study abroad or do a student exchange.
• School is what you make it, the effort you put into your schoolwork will determine how well you do.
• Be accepting to others no matter how different they are

Dear Future Student,

College is definitely a journey that may not necessarily be easy, and you will definitely cry at some point throughout that journey, but finishing your degree will be more than worth it. I started out with a 0.4 GPA because I was dealing with a few personal issues. After being put on academic probation I quickly realized how much my decisions **"then"** would affect me for the rest of my life. So I decided to overcome that and began to excel. I achieved every goal I had and more, including winning a scholarship pageant, joining a sorority, studying abroad, doing a student exchange at an HBCU, multiple internships, and much much more.

I tell all of the students I mentor that college is what you make it. If you don't put in time to study your grades will reflect it. If you don't get involved, you may even feel that you don't fit in. College came with many ups and downs for me, but the best things I took away was learning who I am, building my character, and understanding that everything in life, including obstacles work together for my greater good and make me stronger as long as I don't let the emotions of it weigh me down. I may never even use my degree, but I will use every lesson learned in school. College is a great opportunity, but only you can determine the outcome of your experience.

Kara Hoskins Williams

The University of Texas at Austin
BA, Economics 1996
MA, Leadership 2005
Educator, Entrepreneur

Stop being lazy, Do your work, Study harder

Dear College Self,

Congratulations on getting to UT, but please realize that the time to work has just begun. The study habits that were good enough in high school will not carry over into college. You will have to read the textbook, attend all classes and prepare for your tests in order to succeed. You will need to develop a higher level of discipline and self-control. Fight the urge to slack off and be lazy when your classes require more time and attention than you are used to having to give. You are truly amazing; just do not give up when things get hard.

Listen to your own voice and your own ideas. Don't let your parents choose your major and don't allow them or anyone else to dictate what you do in college. College is the starting point for YOUR future, not theirs. Major in what makes you happy and what makes sense for you. Take advantage of internships, international volunteering opportunities and campus organizations. Live your life YOUR way and do what YOU want to do despite what others say. It's your life. Live it to the fullest!

Signed,
Older and Wiser

"Mr. JB"

__Prairie View A&M University__ (The best HBCU in America)

Education and work is going to fill a large part of your life. Why not do what you love to do and be happy? Don't listen to anybody or anything, but your own heart. This is your journey, not anyone else's. Remember that at the end of it all you will have to live with the decisions you made or even worse didn't make.

Any road you choose will not be easy, and you are going to fail. Nothing worth having is going to be easy to attain. When you fail or fall on the road you chose to travel, fail forward. Learn everything you can from what didn't work and use it in the next effort to try to get just a little closer to that goal. Tune out all the naysayers and family members who cloud your judgement with negative comments like "You've been in college so long, why did you choose that, they don't make any money, or What are you doing with your life?" Listen to that little voice inside you that tells you when and where to move, and move whenever you are good and ready to. Half of those people that have so much to say about your life are living a life someone else created for them, or a job they hate controls. Don't be like them. Don't do the same things over and over expecting different results. Step out on that cliff of life and jump, with the faith that eventually your parachute will open and carry you into the success you always imagined.

Dear**(Insert Your Name Here),**

Thank you so much for reading this book all the way to the end. It brings me great pleasure that a person of your immeasurable value considered my work. It is my hope that you gained something that you can take with you on your own journey and help you get that much closer to reaching those goals. With that being said remember that the speed of your success is solely based on how fast and how often you can implement the knowledge you gain.

Yours Truly,

Jordan T. Ball

Who is Jordan Taylor Ball?

Jordan Ball commonly known to his students as "Mr. JB" is a 24-year-old who was born and raised in Beaumont, Texas. He moved to Houston, Texas at age 15 graduating high school in 2009 at age 17. He then attended Lamar University back home in Beaumont where he soon realized the city had changed from the place he had grown to love.

Next, he chose to re-evaluate his future and developed the life motto "Save the world one laugh, one smile, and one piece of wisdom at a time," where he has fostered all his life decisions to align with his motto. He has volunteered thousands of hours to the development, and mentoring of our next generation of youth through the Boys and Girls Club of America, Local churches, and local mentoring programs.

His path brought him to Prairie View A&M University where he graduated with a Bachelor of Arts in Communications and Chemistry. Jordan Ball has taken on education at the high school and middle school levels in the STEM areas for 2 years, and has been a youth mentor/ minister for the past 7 years since 2009. Working closely with students, other educators, and counselors Mr. Ball has developed an expertise and passion in college readiness for high school students. His passion for inspiring through creativity, relationship, and leadership the future success of our youth has given Jordan the opportunity to help a handful of students. Under his guidance, all of these students have gained full ride scholarship, and financial aid to four-year institutions and hundreds more gained some necessary knowledge that has been used in their successes across the globe.

Some ways other than one on one interaction that Mr. Ball was able to accomplish this goal is by speaking to crowds of sometimes 1000 plus over the past 6 years, and creating multi-media inspirational material. These experiences have helped him cultivate a handbook he uses with students for college readiness and success that has now been made into a book by the name *"Life Hack 101: The Ultimate Guide to College Success".* His future plan is to create a Student Leadership program that will eventually be developed into a private school for all age students. Along with this school, JB plans to continue his niche for public speaking and writing by authoring more books in the coming years, and giving free seminars for students and parents.

Lastly, holding on to the saying that "All things are possible for him who believes it to be so" keeps Jordan Taylor Ball grounded and optimistic toward his future accomplishments.

<u>*I Want To Be*</u>

_____

_____

_____

In the blanks above write down whatever it is YOUR <u>DREAM</u> job or life is. Don't stop at just writing it down. Say this to yourself every single day when you wake up. Jamie Foxx in one of his many interviews after winning his first Oscar stated that a life altering moment in his life was one with none other than Denzel Washington. The only question Jamie Foxx had was, HOW? How did a garbage man from Mount Vernon, New York get here? Where Mr. Washington replied "I had a vision, I wrote down exactly what it is I wanted to be and I meditated on it EVERYDAY!" Learn from these two and many others like Jim Carey, Lady Gaga, or Oprah Winfrey and start creating your tomorrow today. Don't let anybody tell you that you can't do it because all things are possible for them who believe.

Handy Dandy Life Tools

On the following pages, you will find a few things it will be in your best interest to know going forward with your life. Many of the items outlined are things I personally wish they taught our kids in school, but they don't for one reason or another. I may not be an expert in these areas, but I paid attention to what has worked for me along my journey, and researched what a few experts had to say, and put it all together in a comprehensive guide. Take this knowledge, perfect it, and watch how easily success finds you.

Now that you have decided what your legacy will be on

this earth we can put a price on your expertise. On the

next page is a blank check in which you will write to

yourself in the amount that you desire to make for

whatever it is that you want to do in life. *NO AMOUNT IS*

TOO BIG to put out into the universe.

Rules:

- *Date the check for the day in the future you want to achieve this goal. Make it realistic for you!*
- *Put your address and information on the check*
- *Write for services rendered*
- *Take a picture and put it as your screensaver. Make a copy and put it in your wallet until you reach that goal!*

8888

DATE _____

PAY TO THE
ORDER OF _____

$ [ ]

_____ DOLLARS

Law of Abundance Universal Bank

FOR _____

⑆00 000000 ⑈ 000 000 000 000 ⑆ 8888

crystalguidance.com

Life hack 101: The Ultimate Guide to College Success

<u>Just Send Me an email:</u>

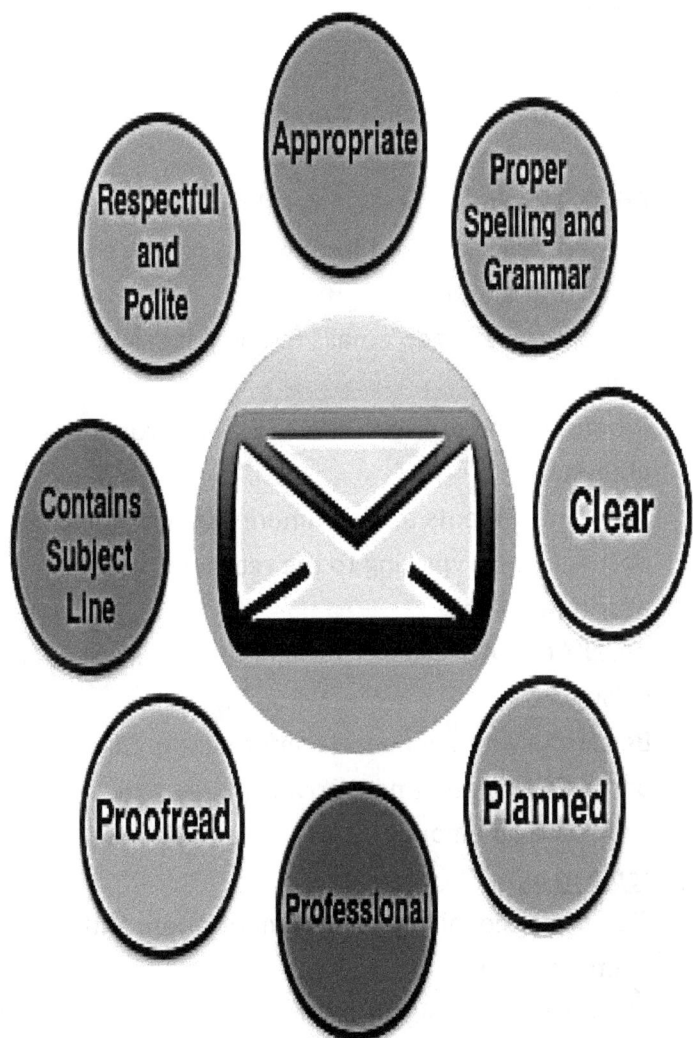

Appropriate

Respectful
and
Polite

Proper
Spelling and
Grammar

Contains
Subject
Line

Clear

Proofread

Professional

Planned

Proper Email Etiquette

- Always have a title line that is clear, concise, and relates to the nature of your email
- Greet the recipient by name
- Briefly introduce yourself. Let the reader know who they are talking to and from where or how they would know the sender
- Try to be brief, keep emails to one page, and get to the point.
- Proofread and use spell check. Ensure proper use of grammar
- Keep attachments to a minimum in amount and size. If necessary give warning to the recipient on large attachments
- ***DON'T USE ALL CAPS***. This signifies you are angry or yelling.
- Be careful with confidential information. Maintain all parties' involved utmost privacy.
- Only send an email to who it is meant for (Be aware of ***reply to all***)
- Stay professional in your communication, and reply in a timely matter
- Always include a signature or farewell. ***(i.e. Thank you in advance, Jane Doe)***

Keys To a Killer Resume

"You will never get a second chance to make a first impression." –Will Rogers-

They Don't Want You To Succeed, But You Got The Keys:

- ✓ **Keep your resume short sweet to the point, focusing on achievements and special talents. (Keep it to 1 page)**
- ✓ *Try to keep it to only jobs and skills that relate to your reason for applying, and the job being applied for.*
- ✓ **Put the most exciting, or unique attributes close to the top of the resume. (I.e. multi-lingual, special certificates or accomplishments)**
- ✓ *Have an eye catching objective that is specific to the company and job including future goals to help improve your desired company/position*
- ✓ **Keep the formatting and design simple but unique (it is ok to experiment with fonts and graphics just keep it professional and to a minimum)**
- ✓ *Have up to date, professional, personal contact information including email address (**NO** nastynate69@hotmail.com)*
- ✓ **Give numbers. (I.e. "I increased sales at my company 50% while I was there, even if that 50% equates to 2 people. Use the number that makes you look best.**
- ✓ *Use keywords*
- ✓ **Be Yourself. You are special I know it, you know it, it's up to you to get the interviewer to see it.**

✓ *Use reverse chronological order. Starting with most recent experiences.*

✓ **Design for the viewer to be able to get the best of you by just skimming over your resume**

✓ *No work experience? Don't worry use relevant and transferrable skills along with any related volunteer or academic projects*

✓ **Always include a relevant and exciting cover letter (Try to keep this to 1 pg. as well)**

✓ *Save it using(first name, last name, Resume)*

Sample Cover Letter

Cover Letter:

Your Name
Your Address
Your Best Contact Phone Number
Your Professional Email
Date
Employer Name *(Specific point of contact name)*
Title
Company
Address
 (Due to formatting this cover letter is more than one page. The original version is 1 page.)

Cover Letter Template - TheInterviewGuys.com

Dear Mr. Sorensen:

When I saw the job posting looking for a Production Office Coordinator for the educational television series, "Wonder Kids," I knew I had to submit my resume. I am a hard-working and enthusiastic Production Office Coordinator with over eight years of practical hands on experience and I'm ready for my next adventure! I am currently looking for an opportunity to continue working within the industry and I know my skills and experiences would be a good fit for the position and the "Wonder Kids" team overall.

As a Production Office Coordinator, my skills include scheduling, contracts, paperwork distribution, and budgeting. I'm also comfortable dealing with vendors, hiring and managing staff, and ensuring the smooth day-to-day operations of a busy office. My experience has included both small and large budget companies, and as a result, I am familiar with the need to be adaptable and find myself excited by the prospect of a challenge.

I am proud of my attention to detail and as a result of my experiences with companies of different sizes and budgets, have been able to develop skills not normally associated with the more traditional Production Office Coordinator role, including graphic design, managing social media and web development. I enjoy working with a wide variety of people and am a multitasker, diligent self-starter and eager team player.

I also wanted to take this opportunity to let you know that my interest in working for you extends beyond my desire to simply be a Production Office Coordinator. I grew up on the show "Wonder Kids" and consider them to be a huge part of my early education. I am a strong believer in quality children's programming and have always felt that "Wonder Kids" provided not only entertainment, but educational value as well. If hired, I would be proud to be a part of the "Wonder Kid" family and help continue that legacy for future generations.

Thank you for taking the time to review my resume and consider me for this position. You can contact me with any questions by emailing me at email@address.com or by calling me at 555-555-5555. I would also love if you could take a look at my website, blancheoatmeal.com.

I look forward to the possibility of discussing this exciting opportunity with you.

Warmest regards,

Blanche D. Oatmeal

"The resume focuses on you and the past. The cover letter focuses on the employer and the future. Tell the hiring professional what you can do to benefit the organization in the future. (12)"
— Joyce Lain Kennedy, Cover Letters for Dummies-

Ten Interview Commandments:

I.   *Thou shall dress appropriately for the interview (research uniforms, colors, dress style of the company.)*

II.   *Thou shall always make eye contact (be aware of wandering eyes)*

III. *Thou shall have a firm proper handshake (Yes, even women)*

IV.   *Thou shall maintain great posture, and body language*

V.   *Thou shall research the employer and be able to relate personal experiences and beliefs to that of the company*

VI.   *Thou shall BE EARLY! (aim for 10-20 min early)*

VII. *Thou shall have questions relating to your possible future with the company not including pay.*

VIII. *Though shall turn off thy cell-phone*

IX.   *Though shall not be complete without a smile*

X.   *Though shall follow up with thanks, and inquiry*

Interview Extra Credit:

☆ Make a great first impression. Your first impression is usually the lasting one so make it memorable in a positive way

☆ Check and stay on top of hygiene (breath, body odor, no over bearing cologne or perfume, clean teeth, manicure face, hair, and nails.)

☆ Keep an extra copy of your resume in a nice folder

☆ A great interview time to aim for is 10:30 AM on Tuesday

☆ Research your interviewer if possible and ask about anything relevant that interest you

The Deal Maker Handshake

A Fortune 500 CEO once said that when he had to choose between two candidates with similar qualifications, he gave the position to the one with a better handshake.

1. Always use your right hand. Make sure it is free, to avoid last minute fumbling.
2. Make sure your hands are warm and dry, not sweaty, clammy, or cold.
3. Stand up and if you are seated when shaking a person's hand, man or woman.
4. Be sure to make eye contact, and give a warm, gentle smile.
5. Angle your thumb straight up to the ceiling, and keep it perpendicular. Never go palm down or palm up.
6. Open your palm wide and don't clasp until the web of your thumbs and palms meet, to ensure maximum contact.
7. Try to wrap your fingers around your partners hand, lock your thumb and squeeze firmly, about as much as your partner does, and lightly shake from the elbow.

the **TEN** most common interview questions

---

1. tell me about yourself

2. why are you suitable for this job

3. why do you want to work at this company

4. why do you want to leave your current job

5. what is your biggest strength

6. what is your biggest weakness

7. where do you see yourself in [x] years

8. what are your salary expectations

9. tell me about a time when you had to work with a difficult person

10. tell me more about [anything on your resume]

www.prepary.com

Why Do You Want To Work For Us? (Cheat Sheet)

From www.themuse.com

Can you tell me a little about yourself?

This question seems simple, so many people fail to prepare for it, but it's crucial. Here's the deal: Don't give your complete employment (or personal) history. Instead give a pitch—one that's concise and compelling and that shows exactly why you're the right fit for the job. Start off with the 2-3 specific accomplishments or experiences that you most want the interviewer to know about, and then wrap up talking about how that prior experience has positioned you for this specific role.

Sample Answer:

"Well, I'm currently an account executive at Smith, where I handle our top performing client. Before that, I worked at an agency where I was on three different major national healthcare brands. And while I really enjoyed the work that I did, I'd love the chance to dig in much deeper with one specific healthcare company, which is why I'm so excited about this opportunity with Metro Health Center."

What do you consider to be your weaknesses?

What your interviewer is really trying to do with this question—beyond identifying any major red flags—is to gauge your self-awareness and honesty. So, "I can't meet a deadline to save my life" is not an option—but neither is "Nothing! I'm perfect!" Strike a balance by thinking of something that you struggle with but that you're working to improve. For example, maybe you've never been strong at public speaking, but you've recently volunteered to run meetings to help you be more comfortable when addressing a crowd.

Sample Answer:

"Well, I used to be pretty horrible at public speaking. When I started college, it was a massive problem, and I was just terrified of doing it, and I didn't do a very good job. So first I took the small step of promising myself that I would speak up in front of really small groups, for example in class. Then, I worked up to taking a public speaking class, which made a big difference. Now, even though I get nervous, I feel like it's something that doesn't completely hold me back, and, in fact, recently I gave a speech at a conference to over 100 people. My hands were shaking the whole time, but I got really good feedback at the end."

Now, let's practice what we just learned:

You are interviewing for a chance at your dream job! Good Luck!

Tell me about yourself?

_____

_____

_____

_____

_____

_____

_____

_____

_____

_____

What do you consider your greatest weakness?

_____

_____

_____

_____

_____

_____

_____

_____

_____

Continue to practice these answers until you memorize them

and are able to say them in a way that does not sound

rehearsed!

Better Understanding Income Taxes

Income Tax is not free money from the government at the end of the year. It is an over payment, or charges for underpayment of taxes paid on the wages the taxpayer made through the taxed year

Tax Facts:

☆ This information is the same information that will be used on your FAFSA for financial aid.

☆ As a dependent for maximum refund your yearly income should stay around $10,000

☆ There is up to a $1,000 education credit awarded for students of at least 6 hours for the tax year up to 4years

☆ If you are a dependent that plans on filing separately from your guardian check with your guardians on the education credit because qualifying you for the credit could disqualify them and cause them to pay more in taxes

☆ If you are a student who marries another student before you both are of the age 24 you could qualify for more financial aid

☆ EIN= Employer Identification Number

☆ Be aware of deadlines First day of tax filing is _____, Last day of tax filing without penalty is _____?

☆ Save all of your tax information over the years. You never know if or when you may need it

☆ Keep this information confidential

American Opportunity Credit

Lifetime Learning Credit

Tuition and Fees Deduction

Do You Want A Million Dollars?
$1,000,000

HOW MUCH YOU NEED TO SAVE EACH DAY TO HAVE $1,000,000 AT 65

STARTING AGE	3% RETURN	5% RETURN	7% RETURN
20	$29	$16	$9
25	$35	$21	$12
30	$44	$29	$18
35	$56	$39	$27
40	$74	$55	$40
45	$100	$80	$63
50	$145	$123	$103
55	$235	$211	$189

BUSINESS INSIDER

Invest that refund check. Let that money make you money!

"The journey to a million dollars begins with one dollar."
The Big "I"

Interest plays a big role in a savings plan. Make sure you shop around to get the best bang for your buck! Below is an Illustration of how interest accrual can be your best friend. Ben saves early and has to put less of his money in and lets the banks interest do the rest. On the other hand, Arthur gets a late start and ends up having to put in more for less.

AGE	BEN INVESTS:		ARTHUR INVESTS:	
19	2,000	2,240	0	0
20	2,000	4,749	0	0
21	2,000	7,558	0	0
22	2,000	10,706	0	0
23	2,000	14,230	0	0
24	2,000	18,178	0	0
25	2,000	22,599	0	0
26	2,000	27,551	0	0
27	0	30,857	2,000	2,240
28	0	34,560	2,000	4,749
29	0	38,708	2,000	7,558
30	0	43,352	2,000	10,706
31	0	48,554	2,000	14,230
32	0	54,381	2,000	18,178
33	0	60,907	2,000	22,599
34	0	68,216	2,000	27,551
35	0	76,802	2,000	33,097
36	0	85,570	2,000	39,309
37	0	95,383	2,000	46,266
38	0	107,339	2,000	54,058
39	0	120,220	2,000	62,785
40	0	134,646	2,000	72,559
41	0	150,804	2,000	83,506
42	0	168,900	2,000	95,767
43	0	189,168	2,000	109,499
44	0	211,869	2,000	124,879
45	0	237,293	2,000	142,104
46	0	265,768	2,000	161,396
47	0	297,660	2,000	183,004
48	0	333,379	2,000	207,204
49	0	373,385	2,000	234,308
50	0	418,191	2,000	264,665
51	0	468,374	2,000	298,665
52	0	524,579	2,000	336,745
53	0	587,528	2,000	379,394
54	0	658,032	2,000	427,161
55	0	736,995	2,000	480,660
56	0	825,435	2,000	540,579
57	0	924,487	2,000	607,688
58	0	1,035,425	2,000	682,851
59	0	1,159,676	2,000	767,033
60	0	1,298,837	2,000	861,317
61	0	1,454,698	2,000	966,915
62	0	1,629,261	2,000	1,085,185
63	0	1,824,773	2,000	1,217,647
64	0	2,043,746	2,000	1,366,005
65	0	**$2,288,996**	2,000	**$1,532,166**

Forbes 7 Best Money Saving Tips:

1. Know what you are working with. (Create a detailed budget and spreadsheet)
2. You don't always have to say yes. (Stay home and save money)
3. Understand your money pitfalls (Shoe budget, Food budget, Going out…
4. Automatically draft and save money where you can't see it (Ira's, Mutual Funds, and Complicated Savings Acct.)
5. Get Organized
6. Set Financial Goals
7. You aren't too young to start saving towards retirement or college

Let's have fun saving money!

➢ ***2 Liters of dimes:*** Use an empty 2-liter bottle to hold spare dimes. Once the bottle is full you will have roughly $600!

➢ ***5 Dollar Challenge:*** Every time you have a 5$ bill at the end of the day fold it up and put it into a jar and save them until the end of the year.

➢ ***Spare Change Challenge:*** Imagine if instead of losing or falling in between seats of your car at the end of the day you put all the change from your transactions throughout the day into a bucket. How much would that bucket be worth in A Month? A Year? 5 Years?

.80cents/day for 1yr. = $292

CHALLENGE ACCEPTED

www.ingramcontent.com/pod-product-compliance
Lightning Source LLC
Chambersburg PA
CBHW060009050426
42448CB00012B/2678